## Praise for *The Strength of Talent*

"Mike Goldman cuts through the noise with a framework that's as practical as it is powerful. Whether you're trying to retain top performers, level up your team, or make tough calls with clarity and compassion, this book gives you the tools to lead with purpose and impact. It's a must-read for any leader serious about growing their people to grow their business."

**DR. MARSHALL GOLDSMITH,** Thinkers50 #1 executive coach and *New York Times*–bestselling author of *The Earned Life*

"Everyone talks about leadership development as a principle, but *The Strength of Talent* teaches it as a set of actionable practices. This book has crystal clear instructions and a proven system that any executive team can deploy to help its people perform at a higher level to where the company is guaranteed to succeed as a by-product."

**RORY VADEN,** *New York Times*–bestselling author of *Take the Stairs* and cofounder of Brand Builders Group

"*The Strength of Talent* is a game changer for any leader who truly believes that developing your people is a core leadership responsibility. One thing I particularly love, and wish I'd had as a submarine commander, is his process for measuring talent density—a leading indicator of business health. If you want to build a business that lasts, this book is for you."

**L. DAVID MARQUET,** former nuclear submarine commander and author of *Turn the Ship Around!*

"Mike Goldman's Talent Density System equips leaders with the tools to assess team performance objectively, develop talent intentionally, and make tough calls confidently. It's the accountability framework today's CEOs need to drive transformative leadership growth."

**TODD MILLAR,** president and CEO of TEC Canada

"If you want to build a team that truly delivers, *The Strength of Talent* is your playbook. Mike Goldman cuts through the noise, showing you exactly how to grow your people and have the conversations that matter most. Pure practicality, endless impact."

**PHIL M. JONES,** author of *Exactly What to Say*

"Mike Goldman delivers a compelling road map for leaders who understand that people—not processes—are the most valuable asset in any organization. This book is packed with real-world stories, hard-earned insights, and an actionable framework that will help you grow your people."

**ANTON J. GUNN**, MSW, CSP, former senior advisor to US President Barack Obama and CEO of 937 Strategy Group

"Mike Goldman tackles a defining challenge of our time: How can leaders effectively strengthen talent in their organizations? With Boomers retiring, Millennials rising, and the talent gap widening, the stakes are high. This book answers the vital question 'How?' not with theory, but with real-world tools rooted in experience."

**KEITH CUPP**, president and CEO of Gravitas Impact Premium Coaches

"*The Strength of Talent* is the quintessential guide on how to spot, nurture, and develop talent. This is a must-read that will help you fall back in love with your business."

**OWEN FITZPATRICK**, psychologist and author of *Inner Propaganda* (forthcoming)

"*The Strength of Talent* is a must-read for any leader wanting to drive growth AND create a fulfilling environment for their team members."

**ANTHONY RUSSO**, president of the Commerce and Industry Association of New Jersey

"Mike Goldman is laser-focused on inspiring leaders to run high-performing teams, knowing what that means and how to measure it."

**MARK PETERS**, CEO of Butterball Farms

"Mike Goldman's process will ask you to clearly define the purpose and outcomes from every role and the skills to accomplish them, gaining optimal performance from your organization."

**ALLAN DOW**, president and CEO of Logility

"Mike Goldman has nailed what so many leaders overlook: Your greatest strategy isn't in your systems; it's in your people. *The Strength of Talent* shows you how to grow your people in a way that directly grows your profit."

**AJ VADEN**, CEO and cofounder of the Brand Builders Group and coauthor of *Wealthy and Well-Known*

… THE STRENGTH OF TALENT

# THE STRENGTH

MIKE GOLDMAN

How to Grow Your
People to Grow
Your Profit

# OF
# TALENT

Copyright © 2025 by Mike Goldman

All rights reserved. No part of this book may be reproduced, stored in a retrieval system or transmitted, in any form or by any means, without the prior written consent of the publisher or a license from The Canadian Copyright Licensing Agency (Access Copyright). For a copyright license, visit accesscopyright.ca or call toll free to 1-800-893-5777.

Talent Density® is a registered trademark of Mike Goldman, LLC. All rights reserved.

Cataloguing in publication information is available from Library and Archives Canada.
ISBN 978-1-77458-585-6 (hardcover)
ISBN 978-1-77458-586-3 (ebook)

Page Two
pagetwo.com

Page Two™ is a trademark owned by Page Two Strategies Inc., and is used under license by authorized licensees

Jacket design by Peter Cocking
Interior design by Cameron McKague
Illustrations by Cameron McKague and Fiona Lee
Printed and bound in Canada by Friesens
Distributed in Canada by Raincoast Books
Distributed in the US and internationally by Macmillan

25 26 27 28 29    6 5 4 3 2

strengthoftalent.com

*For my parents, my biggest cheerleaders, who gave me the confidence to believe I could do anything. They were the first ones I called with good news. Although, since mom was a world-class worrier, they waited a little longer to hear anything bad. I miss you both.*

# CONTENTS

We're Doing It Wrong  *1*

**STEP ONE**
# SET EXPECTATIONS
*31*

**STEP TWO**
# ASSESS PERFORMANCE
*59*

**STEP THREE**
# ACT
*81*

**STEP FOUR**
# DRIVE ACCOUNTABILITY
*129*

**STEP FIVE**
# CASCADE
*155*

Now What?  *179*

Acknowledgments  *183*

# WE'RE DOING IT WRONG

**The Problem**

"Mike, when we start working together, we really need to do something about my CFO."

It was the spring of 2021, and I hadn't even officially started working with him and his team yet, but already on our call, the CEO was complaining about his CFO, nonstop.

"What are you waiting for me for?" I said. "It sounds like you already know the right answer?"

"You're right, Mike, but we're talking to private equity firms and banks to raise capital. You can't fire your CFO when you're in the middle of those discussions."

While I didn't necessarily agree, I decided to wait until we started working together to decide if I needed to dive deeper into this with him.

Three months later…

The CFO problem persisted. I pushed. "What are we doing about your CFO? His lack of accountability and leadership is really starting to impact the team."

"I know you're right, Mike. But things are crazy right now. I just have to wait until things calm down."

I'm not sure I've ever seen things "calm down" in a growing company. And I'm not sure I'd want them to! It was beginning to become obvious that my CEO client was looking for any excuse not to act.

Three more months go by...

Not only was the CFO doing a bad job, but two of the best people on his finance team had quit. The people remaining were overworked and under-led. Once again, I raised the issue with the CEO.

"I know, but I really haven't had a serious conversation with him about it yet. Maybe he just needs more coaching?"

It had now been over six months since he told me how big a problem the CFO was (which meant the problem had been going on *much* longer than that) and he still hadn't talked to the CFO about it!

Finally, after fifteen months, the CFO did something so egregious that the CEO fired him on the spot.

So, who would immediately need to take on all the work and responsibilities of the CFO? It got divided between the CEO, who was already overworked, and the decimated finance team. How urgent was it to hire a new CFO? Super urgent. So, what did he do? He rushed to hire a new CFO, without proper due diligence, and made another hiring mistake.

IT WAS 1994, and I was twenty-nine years old and had started working for a company that asked me to build a brand-new department and revenue stream for the business. The first year was amazing. I was excited to build something, learn new skills, and conquer new challenges. For the previous seven years, I had been a management consultant for a company that's now called Accenture. Working as an employee for one company, versus consulting for several, was a new world for me.

One year in, I had built the new department. I was proud of the team I'd built and the revenue we were bringing in. It was now time to manage the new department. That's when the boredom set in. I needed a new challenge. I designed a new job for myself, expanding my responsibilities beyond this one department, including a promotion of course, and presented my proposal to the CFO (my boss at the time). The response? "Not right now"—we weren't growing enough as a company to warrant the new role.

About a month later, it was time for my annual performance review. The overriding message was "Keep up the good work." Really? I've gotten better advice from a fortune cookie. I was thirty years old and I wanted to grow. I needed a new challenge. Where could I improve? What were my growth opportunities? What should my next focus be? "Keep up the good work" was not good enough. I decided to look for my next job.

IT WAS 2017, and one of my clients was having a constant challenge with drama in the office. There seemed to be a never-ending battle between teams, and even between members on the same team. It impacted their sanity, as well as the team's and its members' ability to grow. Morale was low, employee turnover was high, and everyone was frustrated. At times the place seemed like a high school with different cliques.

In the quarterly planning meetings, there was little time to discuss new plans and strategies for growth. Instead, the focus became fire drills and morale issues. In fact, the CEO had started to doubt he even wanted to grow the business. A bigger business would mean more complexity and drama. Was it worth it?

IT WAS NOVEMBER 2022, and I was in my first two-day planning session with the leadership team of a new client. One of my objectives was to get the team to think more strategically, but every time we dove into defining their new company vision, two of the team members would grind the conversation to a halt. They couldn't see past their current, tactical problems to focus on what they wanted to create in the next three years. We'd go from discussing what new markets they could profitably enter to a discussion of a conversation they needed to have with an angry client later that day.

At lunchtime on day one, the CEO and COO pulled me aside. "Mike, we need to refocus over the next day and a half. Let's just try

**The #1 driver of profit growth** is people growth.

to tackle more tactical issues. We have the wrong team in the room to discuss our vision and strategy."

I agreed and we had some semi-productive tactical discussions. But we never got to the main point of our session together. The new company vision and strategies had not been decided upon. And, without those decisions, they were stuck, focused on the day-to-day, without any real progress to build a stronger, more profitable, more sustainable company.

WHAT DO THESE stories have in common?

They each point to the impact of an inadequate focus on building the strength of talent within our organizations. Three of them are examples of the struggle leaders go through every day when their team members are not performing at the level required to grow a profitable business. One of them is an example of what happens when a high performer is not given the chance to grow.

I spent fourteen years of my life as a management consultant for Accenture and Deloitte Consulting. I'm embarrassed to admit to the dozens of projects and many millions of dollars my clients spent... only to see new visions and strategies implemented poorly or not at all because their teams didn't have the necessary skills or behaviors to drive success.

When I started coaching leadership teams back in 2007, I initially struggled with the same problem. I'd have strong planning meetings with the team, but when I'd see them three months later, very little of what we'd discussed was actually implemented. I struggled with this for over a year, wondering if I was just a bad coach.

Then one day, I was having a coaching call with the CEO of one of the leadership teams. We were discussing her frustration with one of her team members. I decided to broaden the conversation and challenged her to assess the performance of each of her direct reports. Two were performing at a high level, one was doing a solid—but not great—job, one was not producing results, and another was constantly blaming and not taking ownership. That didn't sound like a recipe for success. I asked her what actions she was committed to taking for each member of the leadership team. Who needed coaching? Who needed a greater challenge? Who did she need to coach out of the organization?

For the next six months, that was our focus. Not vision or strategy, but growing the strength of talent on her leadership team. Although we didn't change the world in six months, we absolutely saw company performance increase, while the CEO's frustration decreased. I dramatically increased my focus on leadership team strength of talent with my other clients and saw similar results.

That's when I realized that *the #1 driver of profit growth is people growth*.

A great strategy with the wrong people will fail every time. A mediocre strategy with the right people will succeed every time... as the team learns and adjusts. Peter Drucker once said, "culture eats strategy for breakfast." Well, I believe the strength of talent eats them both.

From that realization, and with the help of my clients over the last fifteen years, I've built the Talent Density System.

This system was born from the pain of leaders facing multiple challenges:

- Struggling to grow their company profitably
- Feeling frustrated that it's hard to find great people
- Feeling frustrated that it's hard to keep great people
- Feeling frustrated that their leaders are not effectively developing their people
- Thinking, "Maybe I'm not cut out for this"
- Thinking, "Maybe growth isn't worth it"
- Feeling overwhelmed that they need to come up with all the answers

We start to fall out of love with our business. We start to dread getting out of bed in the morning. And if we feel that way, how do you think our teams feel? We might think we're hiding the overwhelm and the stress, but our teams see it and feel it too.

It was born out of leaders seeking answers to complex questions:

- How can I find the time to develop people when I don't even have time to get my real work done?
- Shouldn't people be motivated enough to develop themselves?
- What do I do if people don't do what they say they'll do? I can't just fire everyone, can I?
- Why is developing people so important? Why can't I just hire great people and then let them manage their own development?
- How do I keep great people when there's no loyalty anymore?
- What actions can I take to improve the performance of my team members?
- What if we spend all this time developing people and then they leave?
- How can I continue to challenge and develop my highest performers?

These questions can only be answered with an effective framework and process to assess talent, coach talent, develop talent, and know when it's time to transition someone out of the organization who's not a strong fit.

I wrote this book for leaders, but it's also a game changer for our team members. For many, the performance management process can feel like a black box. Our team members often are:

- Confused about what's expected of them
- Surprised by feedback they're given on annual and quarterly performance reviews
- Demoralized or defensive about the performance ratings they're given
- Puzzled by suggestions to improve their performance without helpful, specific actions to guide them

In addition, they get very little real-time feedback from leaders who have very little time for them.

If you or your team are feeling any of these pains or asking any of these questions, you may be tempted to throw in the towel: "Growing a great business is too hard, maybe I'll just settle for a good one." Please don't settle.

Instead of giving up, imagine the following:

- Having a team filled with only high performers
- Being surrounded by people who consistently challenge you to be at your best
- Working with people who are just as self-motivated as you
- Giving up feeling like you must always be the smartest person in the room
- Abandoning the need to micromanage low performers who just don't get it
- Having a team that's so effective that your biggest challenge is how high to raise the bar on their next set of goals

## My Promise

I'm an impatient guy. I don't like to wait years, months, or even weeks to see the value of reading a new business book. I want value *now*. And I'm going to assume you might be like me: If you don't get results *now*, you're moving on.

So, here's my promise.

By reading this book, you will reap the following benefits:

- Appreciate the impact of putting a higher priority on assessing, coaching, and developing your direct reports much more frequently
- Know how and when to make the tough decision to transition someone who's not a strong fit out of the organization

**To scale your company,** you first need to scale your people.

- Develop clearer expectations for each of your direct reports
- Assess the performance of your direct reports using those expectations
- Define a clear set of actions for each of your direct reports based on that assessment
- Create a measurable benchmark for the strength of talent on your team so you can assess progress and hold yourself accountable for improvement
- Craft a plan to implement this framework throughout your organization

And by taking these actions, you will strengthen your team, leading to greater opportunities:

- Increased top- and bottom-line growth
- A growing, fulfilling work environment
- Greater value for your clients and other stakeholders
- Increased trust that your team can get the job done, with or without you
- An ability to successfully take on new, exciting opportunities
- An ability to successfully take on greater challenges

I can confidently make this promise because of the work I've done with my clients as a coach and consultant over the last thirty-five years. More specifically, I've honed this Talent Density System with over a hundred and fifty CEOs and leadership teams over the last twelve years. I've done this through my work with coaching clients and CEO peer advisory groups, including Vistage, Entrepreneurs' Organization (EO), Young Presidents' Organization (YPO), Women Presidents Organization (WPO), and MacKay CEO Forums.

> **BURNING QUESTIONS**
>
> **What if I struggle with an action recommended by the book? Should I stop reading the book until I get the action right?**
> No! Don't let perfect be the enemy of good. Wanting to get things "right" before moving on is a recipe for paralysis. This is not a "one and done" process. It's a never-ending journey. For each exercise and piece of the framework, make your best effort to get it 50-60 percent right (congrats if you get further!) and then move on. Things will get easier, more accurate, and more beneficial as you continue to hone this process over several quarters.

### The #1 Driver of Profit Growth Is People Growth

1 = 3.

One superstar equals the productivity of three average performers. Not one. Three. Not two. Three.

That's a key principle that Kip Tindell, cofounder of The Container Store, set out in his book *Uncontainable*. He calls the principle "1 = 3." You've probably seen this in action: High performers are not just slightly more productive than mediocre performers; they're three times as productive.

In fact, I believe there are roles within organizations where the impact of a high performer is much larger than that. For example, think about a member of your senior leadership team. Their impact cascades down through your organization and to your clients and vendors. Depending on their role, their impact could be more like 1 = 10. I've seen great salespeople or programmers have an outsized impact as well.

What does that mean?

It means that investing in people's growth—developing medium-performing team members into high-performing team members and continuing to coach and challenge your superstars—results in massive value. It means there's great merit in coaching people out of the organization if they're not the right fit. And it means you can pay your superstars double what you're paying mediocre team members and still get a greater return on investment.

Now, that just makes sense, right? More high performers result in greater productivity and increased revenue and profits. We don't need a twelve-hundred-person study to tell us that talent drives top- and bottom-line growth, right? Well, just in case you're skeptical, I've got one anyway.

A Boston Consulting Group (BCG) survey of over twelve hundred leaders found that talent magnets, those companies that rated themselves strongest in twenty different leadership and talent management capabilities, increased their revenues 2.2 times faster and their profits 1.5 times faster than the talent laggards, those companies that rated themselves weakest in those areas. In their study titled "The Global Leadership and Talent Index," BCG included six categories of talent management:

1 **Strategy:** "Planning leadership and talent needs over the short and long term, in line with the strategy and aspirations of the company; developing initiatives to meet those needs and tracking and measuring the initiatives"

2 **Leadership and talent model:** "Defining clear leadership competencies specific to the company's strategy and culture, and embedding those competencies in selection, development, promotion, and reward processes"

3 **Talent sourcing:** "Finding leaders and talent, both internally and externally; tailoring employer branding to specific talent pools; managing and developing successors effectively"

4 **People development:** "Systematically nurturing people by providing comprehensive and structured development opportunities, training, and tools"

5 **Engagement:** "Fostering meritocracy and engagement throughout the company, especially among leaders and top talent"

6 **Culture:** "Requiring top leaders to take responsibility for leadership and talent management by adhering to corporate values"

On the chart based on the BCG survey, you can also see that at each successive level of performance, revenues rose by an average of 15–20 percent and profits by 5–15 percent. While the correlation between talent management and company performance is intuitive, BCG has broken it down and quantified it.

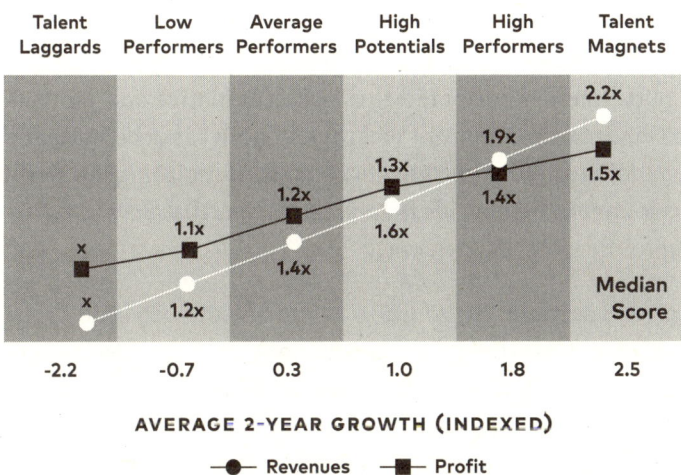

Source: BCG Global Leadership and Talent Index Survey (1,263 Respondents); BCG Analysis

What other initiative can give you that kind of return on investment?

It's also important to understand the impact of low performers on your team. A study was conducted by Eagle Hill and the results published in an article titled "Are Low Performers Destroying Your

Culture and Driving Away Your Best Employees?" The survey of the seventeen hundred professionals from across federal, private, and nonprofit sectors, as well as from various job levels within their institutions, showed that low performers can negatively affect organizations in a number of ways:

**Hurt workplace morale:** "The number one issue was that low performers lowered overall workplace morale (68 percent). Forty-four percent of respondents felt that low performers also increased the work burden on high performers. In addition, respondents felt that managers were spending a disproportionate amount of time managing weaker employees, drawing leadership's attention away from other efforts to support employees and move the organization forward."

**Stifle innovation:** "Over half of respondents (54 percent) felt that low performers contributed to a lack of initiative and motivation, resulting in a work culture where mediocrity is accepted. Survey respondents said that the greatest benefit of replacing low performers is found in the new ideas and approaches that new hires would bring to the work (39 percent)."

**Increase attrition:** "In addition to the obvious attrition drivers—limited career growth (33 percent) and pay (23 percent)—26 percent of respondents within high turnover organizations cited 'poor management' as the primary reason why people leave the organization. In work environments where high-performing employees left more often than low-performing employees, poor management was nearly twice as likely to be listed as the main reason people left (20 percent versus 12 percent)."

The 1 = 3 philosophy, the BCG study, the Eagle Hill study, and my experience over thirty-five years as a consultant and coach have proven that *to scale your company, you first need to scale your people.*

When our business is struggling with dollar growth, as leaders, we tend to decrease our focus on people growth. We focus on the next new idea. We focus on a new strategy, a new product, a new service. There's nothing wrong with that focus, but the most direct line to improving performance, and thereby improving profitability, is growing your people. After all, a higher-performing, more resilient team is exactly what you need to come up with that new strategy, new product, or new service. A higher-performing team is also more likely to execute successfully on those new ideas.

Talent and profit are inexorably linked together in the Talent-Profit Cycle. This can be either a vicious cycle spiraling down to lower profits and lower-performing team members or a virtuous cycle of ever-growing profit and talent.

Here's how the vicious cycle works:

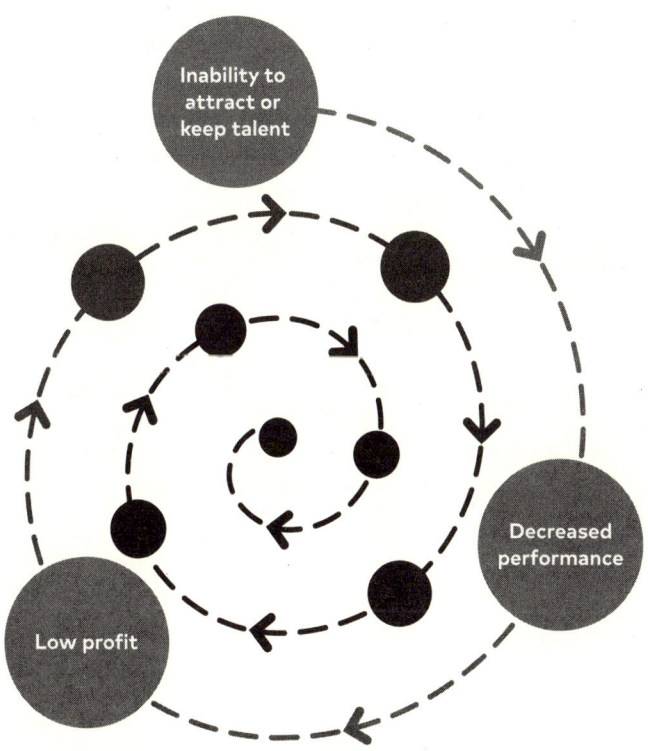

**VICIOUS CYCLE**

1. Inadequate investment (time, money, or skill) in talent development leads to an inability to attract or retain high performers.
2. The lack of high performers leads to decreased company performance.
3. Decreased performance leads to lower profits.
4. Lower profits reduce the ability to invest in or provide opportunities for high performers, hurting the ability to attract and retain them.
5. The ever-decreasing number of high performers drives even lower company performance.
6. Decreased company performance leads to even lower profits.
7. And so on…

That sounds like every CEO's nightmare. So, let's better understand the virtuous cycle:

1. Significant investment (time, money, and skill) in talent development leads to a powerful ability to attract and retain high performers.
2. A high number of high performers leads to increased company performance.
3. Increased company performance leads to higher profits.
4. Higher profits enable a greater ability to invest in, or provide opportunities for, your highest performers, strengthening your ability to attract and retain them.
5. The ever-increasing number of high performers drives even greater company performance.
6. Increased company performance leads to even higher profits.
7. And so on…

## VIRTUOUS CYCLE

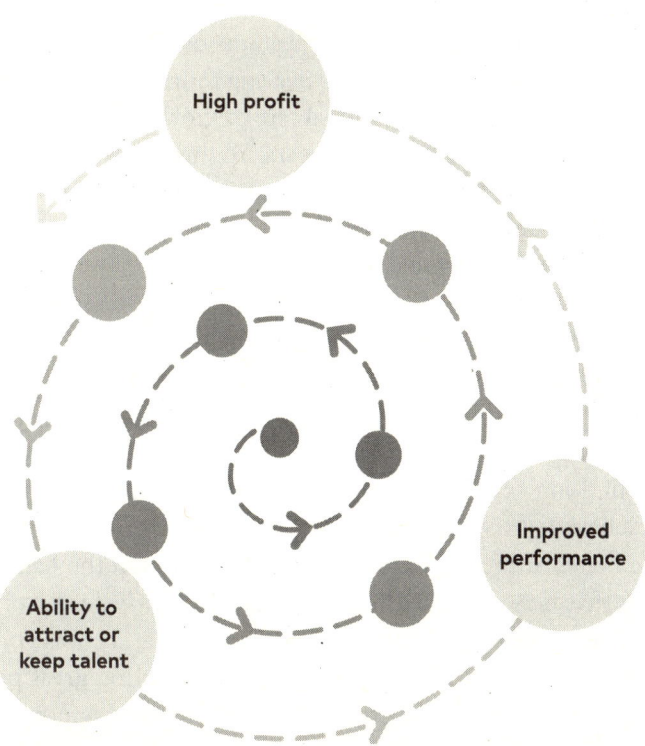

High-performing team members want more interesting challenges, more responsibility, more opportunity, and more growth. If they can't find that at your company, they'll find it somewhere else.

Notice in my description of the Talent-Profit Cycle, I haven't included stable performance (not growing or shrinking) as an option. That's because I haven't seen a company with flat revenue growth and low profitability stay that way very long. In time, an organization in that situation still begins to lose its ability to attract and retain great people who want to grow and thrive. At that point, it will either find a way to start to grow, and enter the virtuous cycle, or not, and enter the vicious cycle. Either you're growing or you're dying.

Here's an interesting example of the Talent-Profit Cycle in action, although turned on its head a bit.

I was talking to a CEO about the status of his business and the challenges he was having. He was nearing retirement and was satisfied with the 2 to 3 percent annual rate of growth his business had been achieving over the last five years. You might ask, "Why is he satisfied? Shouldn't he be striving to grow faster than that?" Maybe, but it's his business and his life. If 2 to 3 percent growth makes him happy, who am I to argue with that? Except...

After he shared his modest growth goals, he communicated his constant frustration with his team and the state of the workforce.

"There are just no good people out there! I post a job, and I hear crickets." "These millennials want everything handed to them. Why don't they work hard like I did when I was their age?" "When I finally find someone good, they leave for another opportunity. Don't people have loyalty anymore?"

He believed the problem was "out there," when the harsh reality was that he was just seeing the Talent-Profit Cycle at work. As long as he was happy growing 2 to 3 percent a year, he was going to have a tremendous challenge keeping and attracting great people. Slow top- and bottom-line growth meant infrequent opportunities for his people to grow. They weren't being challenged. Promotions were rare. And he had little ability to invest in coaching and development.

So, he had two choices. He could continue having low growth goals and continue the frustrations with his team and the workforce, or he could strive to grow more aggressively. He could define some bigger, more powerful goals for his organization.

> **BURNING QUESTIONS**
>
> **Isn't strategy more important than people development?**
> Strategy is important, of course. But the best strategy implemented by a mediocre team will fail miserably. On the other hand, if your strategy is ineffective, a great team will figure that out early, change course, execute with discipline and find success anyway. People trump strategy... every time.
>
> **Why is developing people so important? Why don't I just hire great people and then leave them alone?**
> I believe there are many "great people" that perform at a mediocre level because they're not effectively being challenged, coached, motivated, or held accountable. We hire people with the potential to be great. As leaders, it's our responsibility to help our team members realize that potential.

## Why Performance Management Doesn't Work

The "performance management process" is at the heart of people development. In most companies, this includes things like training, goal setting, rating and ranking systems, coaching, and the dreaded annual performance review (more on this horrible process later).

But here's the problem.

In the 2019 Mercer "Global Performance Management Survey," only 2 percent of companies interviewed believed that their performance management approach delivered exceptional value. Two percent!! If the #1 driver of profit growth is people growth, this is a very scary statistic. Our people growth processes are not working!! But why?

### Inadequate Measures of Individual and Team Performance

For most functions, our measures of performance are anecdotal, inaccurate, or nonexistent. We incentivize the wrong things. There are some exceptions, like salespeople having a measure based on new revenue. But how we measure individual and team performance is scattered at best.

For example, one way many human resources functions are measured is on the time it takes to hire someone. Should hiring someone quickly be a measure of success? I hope not. Should implementing a new training program be a measure of success? Not when most training programs add little or no value.

Another great example is marketing. Is a marketing function successful if the new website is implemented on time? If the new logo looks really good? If we get a ton of clicks on our new email campaign? I'd argue that marketing can do all those things and still be dramatically unsuccessful. If the new website, new logo, new email marketing campaign doesn't result in qualified leads that sales can close, where's the value?

In the past, before remote and hybrid work were the norm, people incorrectly measured productivity based on how hard it looked like someone was working. Or how many hours they were working. I can remember working many years ago for a CFO who was always in the office on weekends. There were weekends I came in just to show my face, even though I really didn't have any work to do. But I wanted to show him I was working hard.

That's obviously not the right way to measure performance. And it became even more clear that it was the wrong way to measure performance when remote and hybrid work came into play. We realized we needed some true ways to measure performance since we couldn't actually see how hard or long our people were working.

### Culture Fit Is an Afterthought

Very often, the words "performance" and "productivity" are used interchangeably. But they're not the same thing. Productivity is about progress toward hitting quantifiable measures of success like sales, client retention, or timely deliveries. I believe performance is about more than that and should also include culture fit. In fact, very often culture fit is a more important measure for two reasons. First, productivity is much more coachable than culture fit (more on that in Step 3). Second, someone that's a poor culture fit impacts their own performance as well as the performance of the team members around them.

Though culture fit may not be part of how performance is measured in most organizations, it's certainly discussed. However, with no clear measure of culture fit, identifying culture fit issues and taking effective action is weak.

**Poor Coaching and Development Skills**

Many of our leaders have no idea how to be great coaches. In fact, most don't know the difference between coaching, development, and accountability. And even if they did know, they don't have the time to have one-on-one meetings with their direct reports regularly.

We substitute true coaching and development with elaborate training programs. While some training programs add great value, many are ineffective because they assume we all learn the same way and are at the same level of development. They also assume that if our team members learn something, they'll be able to effectively execute on what they learned. Without effective coaching, mentoring, and follow-up (things they don't make time for), the learning is soon forgotten, and the training time and dollars are wasted.

We also substitute coaching and development with annual performance reviews. I believe the annual performance review is the worst business invention ever. Imagine being on a sports team and your coach waits until the end of the season to give you critical feedback to improve your performance. It makes no sense! And if you're smiling because you do quarterly performance reviews... congratulations, you execute this horrible process four times per year. We'll review what should replace this process in Step 3.

**Little or No Leadership Accountability for People Growth**

It's popular to say "people are responsible for managing their own careers"—popular and partially true. But as leaders, we need to take responsibility as well. I can't think of a more important role for a leader than to strengthen the talent and performance on their teams. And yet, we do very little to hold leaders accountable for this... until annual performance review time.

Part of the reason we do such a poor job of holding leaders accountable for people growth is that we have no way to measure it. I'll say more about this in Step 4.

## The Three Characteristics of a Great Company

Before diving deeper, let's zoom out to discuss the bigger picture. If the goal of great performance is to create a great company, we need to know what a great company is. I find there are three characteristics of a great company:

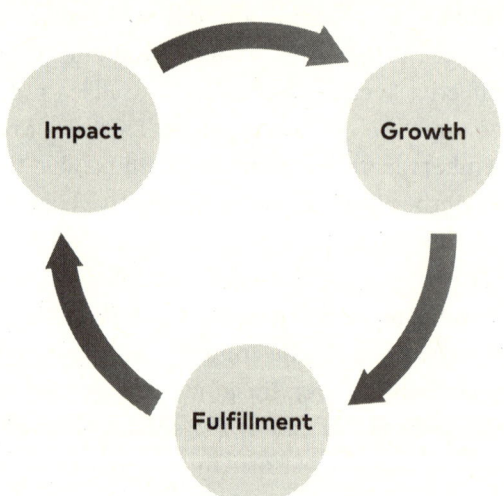

1 **Consistent and significant top- and bottom-line growth.** If you're not growing, you're dying. We need growth not only to keep the company alive but also to continue to invest in people, process, and systems.

2. **A growing, fulfilling environment.** It's not just about the numbers; it's about the environment you create. If you're at a high-growth company but you wake up every morning and dread going to work, you don't have a great company. I also think your growth won't last very long if people don't feel fulfilled by their work and if they're not consistently being challenged with exciting opportunities and interesting challenges.

3. **Significant impact on the world.** This doesn't mean that to be a great company you need to be feeding the hungry or ending climate change. By world, I mean your world. The world of your client, team members, and vendors. If you're not adding significant value, you're not a great company.

This is how I define a great company. Your definition may be different. That's okay. The critical point is that the expectations you set for your team members should drive toward that definition.

## Introducing the Talent Density System

As leaders we need to get better at measuring talent, we need to get better at developing talent, and we need to get better at holding our leaders accountable for measuring and developing talent.

We need a framework. We need something better than the tools we've lived with for decades. We need a framework to help us better assess talent, develop talent, coach talent, and make the tough decisions as to whether they even belong on the team.

We need a framework that helps us build the strength of talent, which I define as *the power of building a team of the right people doing the right things.*

The *right people* means people who behave in a way that aligns with the company's desired culture and helps make the people around them better.

The *right things* means people who produce results that effectively drive the company toward its vision.

For the remainder of this book, I'll guide you through a process that will help you build the strength of talent. I call it the Talent Density System, and I've built and honed it with my clients over the last twelve years.

The phrase "talent density" has been used before. However, it tends to be loosely defined as a percent of top performers in your organization. This assumes there is a standard "top performer" definition. It also doesn't consider the impact low performers have on an organization (I'd rather have 60 percent top performers and 40 percent mediocre performers than 70 percent top performers and 30 percent low performers). Lastly, it's defined as a measure, not a system or framework, to be implemented. My goal in this book is to go beyond the concept of talent density and guide you through a step-by-step approach as well as a better talent density measure.

Here's an overview of the five-step Talent Density System.

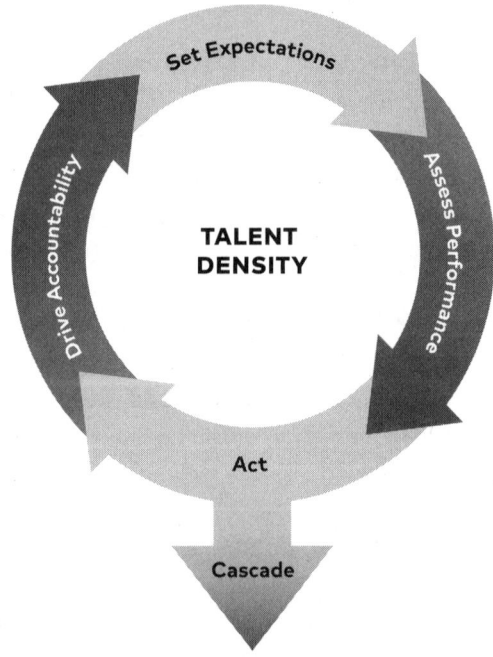

**Step 1: Set Expectations**

Most companies and leaders set unclear expectations or don't set them at all. In this step, I'll introduce the Talent Density Expectations Model to help you understand and practice the right way to set expectations for both the right people and the right things.

**Step 2: Assess Performance**

I'll introduce the Talent Assessment Model and help you use the model to assess the performance of direct reports against expectations. I'll also describe the four categories of performance that will help drive actions to improve the strength of talent on your team.

**Step 3: Act**

I'll detail specific, recommended actions for each of your direct reports. To help you accomplish that, I'll describe the key philosophies that should drive action, specific actions for each level of performance, and more general actions for all levels of performance.

**Step 4: Drive Accountability**

We'll discuss the critical importance of holding leaders accountable for growing the strength of talent on their team. I'll also describe specific ways to hold leaders accountable for taking action and getting results. I'll introduce the quarterly talent assessment meeting (QTAM) as the truth serum and driver of accountability. I'll also introduce the Talent Density Indicator (TDI), a key performance indicator used to benchmark, measure progress, and hold leaders accountable for building their teams' strength of talent. You'll calculate your team's TDI and set goals to help you drive your accountability.

**Step 5: Cascade**

In this step, I will describe a top-down approach to proliferate throughout your organization and recommend actions to manage some obstacles you may encounter when implementing something foundationally new. While you may be excited about this new process and tempted to roll this out to the whole organization, I advise you to take it slow.

Parts of this framework may sound familiar. You may already be executing the steps within the framework... in some way. That's great! It means you have a head start. However, the power of this framework comes from its comprehensive nature. Implementing parts of this process without bringing it all together into a thorough and consistent framework will negate much of what you're trying to achieve.

The power of this framework also comes from the specific distinctions within each step:

- A model that creates consistency in how performance is assessed and frees you from the problems associated with "easy graders" and "hard graders"

- A specific way to "score" culture fit, an area typically too qualitative and subjective

- Sixteen specific actions for leveraging, developing, and retaining high-performing team members

- More consistency and rigor in the process to decide how to handle low-performing team members

- A step-by-step approach to quarterly sessions focused on collaborating, debating, and holding leaders accountable for improving strength of talent

- The creation of a key performance indicator to benchmark the strength of talent, measure progress, and drive accountability

Now let's dive into Step 1, where you'll develop clearer expectations for each of your direct reports.

## BURNING QUESTIONS

**Aren't there other frameworks out there that work as well? What about 9-Box or the EOS People Analyzer?**
While there are other frameworks that strive to help strengthen organizational talent, I've yet to find one that effectively assesses talent, drives specific actions, and holds leaders accountable. As for the 9-Box Grid and the EOS People Analyzer (two of the more popular frameworks I've come across), I believe both are lacking, but for different reasons:

**The 9-Box Grid**
- There is no measure of culture fit, only performance and potential.
- The performance measure is too subjective (low, moderate, high) without any guidance on specific measures of productivity that align with company goals.
- Too much weight is put on potential, which is very subjective and open to misinterpretation.

**EOS People Analyzer**
- While this tool does assess culture fit, I find the + or – for each core value to be overly simplistic.
- The productivity measures of a "yes" or "no" for "Gets It," "Wants It," and "Capacity to Do It" are also overly simplistic and are ineffective measures of true productivity.

Lastly, neither of these frameworks, nor any others I've come across, have a specific key performance indicator focused on strength of talent, and this lack limits their ability to create benchmarks, goals, and accountability focused on people growth.

**I don't see a step focused on hiring in your framework. Is hiring the right people a key part of the process?**
It's absolutely a critical part of the process. However, there are two reasons I'm not including it in the book:

1. There are countless excellent books written about the recruiting and hiring process. I typically encourage my clients to read and follow the process outlined in *Who: The A Method for Hiring* by Geoff Smart and Randy Street. I would recommend this book to you as well.

2. While I agree it's critical to implement a thorough sourcing, recruiting, evaluation, and hiring process, the problem is that we tend to think it's all about hiring. We've either hired right or hired wrong. I believe the reality is that we can dramatically improve the chances of making a hire the right hire through better coaching and development.

### Quick Review

The #1 driver of profit growth is people growth:
- The BCG study showing the massive impact of effective leadership and talent management capabilities
- The 1 = 3 philosophy
- The impact of the Talent-Profit Cycle

Traditional performance management processes have problems:
- Inadequate measures of individual and team performance
- Culture fit is an afterthought
- Poor coaching and development skills
- Little or no accountability for people growth

Great companies have three characteristics:
- Consistent and significant top- and bottom-line growth
- A growing, fulfilling environment
- Significant impact on the world

## Introducing My Five-Step Talent Density System

1. Set Expectations
2. Assess Performance
3. Act
4. Drive Accountability
5. Cascade

Throughout the book, I'll give you access to tools and templates that will help you implement the ideas we'll discuss.

Go to my website strengthoftalent.com to access my book resources, where you'll find the Strength of Talent Toolkit, master class, and community.

STEP 1

# SET EXPECTATIONS

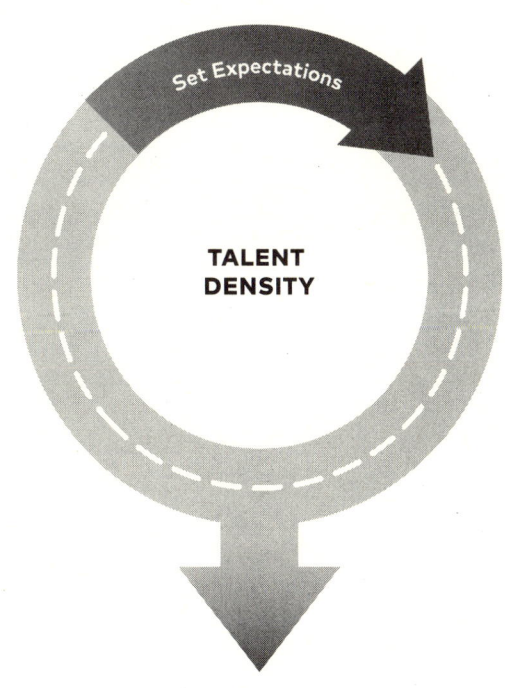

## Setting Expectations—the Wrong Way

We're setting expectations the wrong way... or not setting them at all.

Of course, most organizations set expectations for revenue and profitability. But what about the activities that drive those results? How many marketing-qualified leads will it take to achieve those results? What does our sales win rate need to be? What net cash flow will we need to drive the business? How will we measure client engagement? Not setting expectations and measuring these things is like playing a sport and not knowing the score.

Here are some key mistakes we're regularly making:

### We're Not Measuring the Right Things

Imagine flying an airplane and not knowing your altitude, or your airspeed, or where you are on the map. Most organizations are flying blind.

Sometimes these metrics have been identified but they're not being tracked, or not being tracked accurately. More often, leaders haven't even identified what numbers are important. Even if the right numbers are being tracked, many companies don't have targets or goals in mind for those numbers. Customer service shares client retention numbers and everyone just nods their heads. If there's no goal, what are we supposed to do with those numbers? They need to be actionable.

Success is not about everyone working hard. Success should be quantifiable.

### We're Not Holding People Accountable for Those Measures

Once companies understand how to measure success, many still do a poor job holding people accountable for those measures. There are many reasons for that; however, two of them prevail:

1. There is no consistent process for holding people accountable—no consistent "rhythm" for reviewing the numbers and coming up with action plans when targets aren't being met.

2. Too many people are "accountable." I've seen leadership teams that have three different people accountable for "revenue." Or leaders that say, "We're all accountable for client retention." If everyone is accountable, then no one is accountable.

### We Believe Performance Equals Productivity

As I mentioned previously, most organizations treat "performance" and "productivity" as synonyms. If a salesperson is meeting or beating their sales goals, they're performing successfully. But there's something critical missing from that equation. What if that "high-performing" salesperson is disrespecting members of the customer service team, causing frustration? What if they're not communicating well with their sales manager, causing confusion? Are they still high performing? In one word: no.

### Unclear Expectations Don't Lead to *Unclear* Results— They Lead to *Unacceptable* Results

One of my clients decided to build and sell software products to complement the services they performed for their clients. They believed this would help them add more value to their clients, diversify their revenue streams, and make their business both more profitable and scalable.

Quarter after quarter, they measured success by their ability to deliver these technology products on time and on budget. They defaulted to this measure without much debate. It just seemed logical.

For several quarters, the technology team failed to deliver on this measure of success. Each quarter, more time and money were invested to solve the problem. Finally, by upgrading their technical architecture, outsourcing key technology resources, and improving their project management processes, they began to hit their budgets and timeframes.

Success, right? Wrong!

While they finally delivered the software "successfully," no one bought it! They were so focused on getting the technology right, they spent little time remembering why they were building it in the first place.

After investing hundreds of thousands of dollars, they realized they had the wrong measure of success. Looking back, it might seem obvious that the right measure was return on investment—or, at least, specific revenue goals. But it wasn't obvious to them because they didn't prioritize setting clear expectations early in the process.

Once the client began to focus on revenue and return on investment as the right measures of success, they created a strategy with a much better probability of success. They involved their clients earlier in the process, implemented a more iterative investment model, and created a cross-functional team selling approach. Most importantly, no money was spent without a clear understanding and level of confidence in the return on investment.

That's an example of the impact of a specific initiative with an unclear (or just wrong) measure of success. But the problem is bigger than that. In my experience, many team members are diligently working on efforts that get them, and their company, no closer to success.

- Marketers are spending time on marketing campaigns that aren't driving potential sales.

- Human resources professionals are developing training programs that are not increasing productivity or improving culture.

- Finance professionals are focusing on closing the books faster each month but aren't improving cash flow.

They're working hard without a focus on the right measures of success. Without knowing where the finish line is.

How can we effectively assess performance when we're not sure what effective performance looks like?

## The Right Way: The Talent Density Expectations Model

The right way to measure and assess performance is on two axes: productivity and culture fit.

A team member is highly productive when they're achieving results: when they're meeting or beating their target key performance indicators (KPIs).

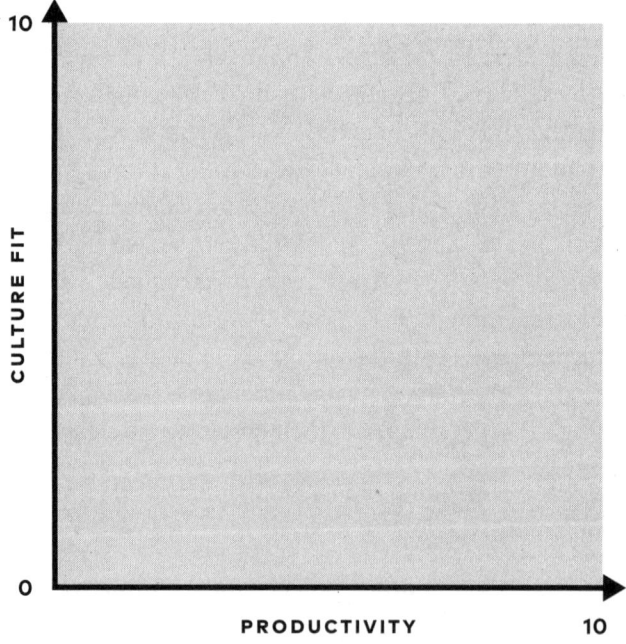

A team member is a strong culture fit when they're making people around them better: when they're living your company's core values.

You might notice there's no third component called "potential." We all have potential. What our business needs is performance. I see leaders use "potential" as an excuse way too often for people that aren't performing. Just because you like someone and think they can perform well doesn't mean they will realize that potential. A leader can discuss potential and use it as motivation to coach and develop. However, the goal is not to measure and assess potential; it's to measure and assess productivity and culture fit. And a strong performer needs to excel at both.

So, how do you know they're excelling? Let's talk about that next... starting with productivity.

## Setting Productivity Expectations

The success of your company is driven by the success of each function within the company. While that sounds logical, there are two problems. Some companies aren't clear on what their functions are. And very few companies effectively measure the success of each function.

To aid my clients with this process, I use the Functional Accountability Chart.

| Functional Accountability Chart | | | |
|---|---|---|---|
| Functions/ Business Units | Accountability | Success KPI1 | Success KPI2 |
| Head of Company | | | |
| Sales | | | |
| Marketing | | | |
| Finance | | | |
| Human Resources | | | |
| Operations | | | |
| Information Technology | | | |
| Customer Service | | | |
| R&D | | | |

As simple as it sounds, the first step in setting productivity expectations is to ensure there is alignment on what the functions/business units are in your company (leftmost column). When I say functions/business units, I don't mean titles. For example, CEO is not a function. VP of sales and marketing is not a function. Just because sales and marketing report to one person doesn't mean it's one function.

True functions include things like head of company, sales, marketing, finance... you get the idea. The example chart I've given contains a generic list as a starting point (most are probably functions in your company). The first step is to customize this list by adding functions or business units, removing ones that don't apply to your organization, and modifying ones named differently—for example, "we don't call it HR, we call it *talent management*." This sounds simple, but when I conduct this exercise with my clients, I find that not all leaders agree on the functions and business units.

The functions in the sample chart assume you're the head of your company, since it lists most of the major functions of a company. If you're the CFO, with a goal of setting expectations for your team, your list should include functions you're accountable for: accounts payable, accounts receivable, financial planning and analysis, etc. If you're the head of operations, your list might include manufacturing, logistics, procurement, etc.

Most leaders have no more than eight to fourteen functions reporting to them. If you find yourself listing out too many functions, you're probably at too low a level of detail.

When you think about these functions, a popular question is "What if I outsource a function? If I outsource a function, that's not a function, right? Because we don't perform that—we outsource it." Wrong. Many small and midsize organizations outsource their IT function. That doesn't mean no one in your organization is accountable for it. Someone needs to be accountable for managing the relationship with the outsourced provider, setting service level requirements, deciding when and if to bring the function back in house, etc.

The second column of the Functional Accountability Chart is accountability. This column answers the question, "Who is the *one* person accountable for this function?" This is the person who owns the function. It is their job to strategize, plan, and manage the performance of this function. One and only one person is accountable. Having more than one person accountable for a function means no one is accountable for that function. Among other problems it causes, it will become difficult to create clear productivity expectations and hold an individual accountable if accountability is "shared."

While having multiple people accountable for one function is a problem, having one person who is accountable for multiple functions is okay and expected... unless it's causing that person to be stretched too thin. In fact, in my book *Breakthrough Leadership Team*,

**Unclear expectations** lead to unacceptable results.

I discuss three questions you should be asking to test your team's structure. I'll summarize them here:

1. **Is more than one person accountable for a function?** For example, you may have three regional heads of sales reporting to the CEO. If three people are accountable, no one is accountable.

2. **Do you have any functions with no one accountable?** For example, everyone in the company may have a responsibility to provide outstanding customer service, but you may not have identified the one person who owns the customer service function.

3. **Is anyone on your team stretched too thin?** A leader may be stretched too thin if they're accountable for too many functions. They may also be stretched too thin if you've defined a function as one thing (administration) when it's really three things (finance, human resources, and facilities). Lastly, they may be stretched too thin when their skills have not scaled to handle the role successfully.

The next step in this process is to create one to three productivity expectations (commonly called measures of success or key performance indicators) for each function. Is your marketing function successful because they created a great-looking new website? Is your HR function successful because they created a new onboarding process or a new performance evaluation process?

When you don't effectively measure the success of a function, you spend time on the wrong things, hire the wrong people, promote the wrong people, and miss out on major opportunities to grow the business. You wonder why it feels like you're working incredibly hard but not seeing results.

You can't gauge the success of a function by how hard anyone is working or the sheer volume of work they're getting done. Functions like marketing, HR, sales, and IT need to be measured by their results and how they impact the business.

For a sales role, it might be new revenue. For an accounts receivable role, it might be days sales outstanding.

But some functions aren't as straightforward.

For example, how do you know if your marketing function is successful? A great place to start is to define the purpose of your marketing function. If marketing's purpose is to drive more leads to your sales function, then the most important measure of success might be the number of inbound qualified leads. That may not be the only measure. Maybe marketing's purpose is also to drive brand awareness. Then you might want to measure the company's social media following or hits to the company website.

Let's explore human resources and consider the purpose of the function. If HR's primary function is to hire and develop high performers, should a key measure be time to hire, or the number of new people hired? That seems to be more about quantity than quality. A better measure might be the percentage of high performers in the organization (I'll share a specific measure for this called the Talent Density Indicator in Step 4 later in the book). Putting in a new recruiting process or a new performance evaluation process does not mean HR is successful. They're only successful if those things drive real results for the company.

If you're struggling to identify the right measure of productivity for a function, here are some questions that may help:

- What's the mission of the role? How does this role contribute to the overall success of the company?

- How do you know if they're succeeding or failing in that mission?

- What would have to happen for them to deserve a promotion?

- What would have to happen for you to want to fire them?

*Productivity is not about how long and hard someone is working.* It may be that they're working so many hours because they're *not* productive. Productivity is about the measurable results they're achieving.

Here are some principles that should help guide you in creating the right productivity metrics.

### Define a Small Number of Metrics
Setting expectations for a team member's productivity using fifteen different metrics is not helpful and often harmful. It's confusing, too much to track, and often the metrics conflict with one another. For setting expectations and assessing productivity, two to four metrics are best.

### Give Each Metric a Target
Define expectations for each metric by setting a specific target. As an example, if marketing productivity will be measured with a KPI of marketing qualified leads, set it to five marketing qualified leads per week.

### Select Higher-Frequency Measures
It's very hard to hold people accountable to annual or quarterly measures. By the time you know there's a problem, it's too late to do anything about it. The best measures are weekly, or monthly. Higher-frequency measures allow for more frequent accountability and coaching.

### Use Both Lagging and Leading Metrics
A lagging metric is the measure of a result, the measure of something that happened in the past. Revenue and gross margin are lagging indicators. A leading indicator is the measure of an activity that drives a future result. New revenue is a lagging measure for a salesperson. A good leading indicator might be the number of sales meetings they're having per week. Leading metrics are critical because they're much easier to impact than lagging metrics. If the business needs a sales increase of 20 percent, you may not know what to do. But If I said go increase your sales meetings by 20 percent, the actions are clearer.

Leading metrics are especially critical when the time from action to result is long. For example, if you're selling enterprise software with a sales cycle of four to six months, just looking at lagging metrics will blind you to the fact that you may be doing all the right things, but you just haven't seen the results yet. This can cause you to change course, thinking you're failing, instead of continuing to drive the actions that will, eventually, lead to strong results.

### "Balance" Your Metrics

Be careful what you ask for. If you define inventory turn as the sole measure of success for your head of operations, you might get amazing inventory turns, but low order fulfillment and customer service because your inventory is too low. If you define new revenue as the sole measure of success for your head of sales, you might get record sales, but lose money because, to hit the new revenue target, sales dropped prices. When defining productivity metrics, use counterbalancing measures where possible: inventory turn *and* order fulfillment, new revenue *and* gross margin.

### "Weight" Your Metrics

Some metrics are more important than others. Let's use marketing as an example. You might identify marketing qualified leads (MQLs), social media engagement, and white papers downloaded as productivity metrics. While they're all important, if the overriding mission of your marketing function is to generate MQLs, that metric should be weighted, and prioritized higher than the other two. At the end of the day, we need to see results. If the leading metrics aren't getting us there, we may need to change our leading metrics.

Which metric is most important can be impacted by a team member's tenure in a role. For example, we might weight leading metrics higher for a new salesperson, depending on the length of our sales cycle. We also might weight leading indicators higher for a new product, service, or business unit. Early on, getting the activities right may be more important than seeing results. Once the salesperson has been in the role awhile, or the new product, service, or business unit has matured, you might change the weighting to give the lagging metrics greater priority.

### Set Expectations Collaboratively

Expectations should be set collaboratively with each of your direct reports. This may lead to a bit of give-and-take, but it's worth it to ensure they own it. When you dictate expectations to a team member, you own the expectations, not them. If they miss a target, they'll blame it on your unrealistic expectations, not their own performance.

### Define Role Success That Drives Company Success

When defining productivity expectations, it's important to ensure that if all team members hit their targets, the company will hit its targets. I know this seems obvious, but it's not always easy. I've seen companies that have a majority of team members hitting or beating their productivity targets, and yet, the company is badly missing their revenue and profitability targets. How can this be? Easy... the metrics, or targets for those metrics, are the wrong ones to drive company success.

### Set Targets That Are Achievable, Yet Realistically High

Productivity targets that are easy to achieve are demotivating and limit your organization's growth. On the other hand, "stretch goals" that seem unachievable are also demotivating. The sweet spot is right in the middle: achievable, yet high enough that it challenges the individual, and your organization, to learn, grow, and be creative.

### Focus on the Role, Not the Person

Focus on the role and what is needed from that role to achieve your organization's vision and goals. Don't lower your expectations because the person in the role can't achieve or hasn't yet achieved them. That includes a new hire, or someone recently moved or promoted into a new role.

We need to remember that the main purpose of this exercise is to ensure we're taking the right actions to improve performance. Lowering expectations would blind us to the key actions we need to take to get them up to speed and up to the level expected of that specific role. A lower performance category for a couple of quarters is not a reflection on them; it's a reflection of the work we need to do together to drive results.

When promoting or changing the role of a high performer, you should expect that they may drop down to medium or low performance for a time. This is not necessarily a reflection on them—they didn't suddenly become a problem team member. Rather, it's the reality that it may take some time to get them performing at the level required for their new role.

### Review Productivity Expectations Periodically

Don't let your productivity expectations get stale. If an individual consistently meets or beats the target, it may be time to raise the bar and set a higher target. If an individual consistently misses a target, it may be time to reassess... the target or the individual. I'd suggest reviewing productivity expectations quarterly and whenever there is a significant "business changing" event.

---

**WHAT TO DO NOW**

Set productivity expectations:

1. List the functions within your organization using the Functional Accountability Chart.
2. Determine the one person accountable for each of the functions.
3. Define your own productivity expectations.
    - Identify two to four productivity metrics of success for your role.
    - Determine the frequency of each of the metrics (weekly, monthly, etc.).
    - Define targets for each measure.

- Discuss and align on the measures with your leader. Adjust as necessary.
- Discuss the measures with your peers to get feedback.
- Review and discuss the measures with your direct reports... for feedback, and to use for determining their own productivity expectations.

4. Define productivity expectations for each of your direct reports based on their functions and accountabilities.
   - Collaborate with your direct reports on two to four productivity metrics of success. This may mean rationalizing metrics if some one is accountable for multiple functions.
   - Determine the frequency of each of these metrics (weekly, monthly, etc.).
   - Define targets for each measure.
   - Meet with each of your direct reports to discuss these measures. Not to dictate to them, but to discuss, get feedback, and adjust as necessary. In time, as you and your direct reports get more comfortable with the process, you may want to give them more ownership. Let them come up with the measures to review with you, rather than you drafting them first.

## BURNING QUESTIONS

**What if I'm struggling to define someone's measurable productivity expectations? Should I stop here and not implement the rest of the process until I get this right?**
No. Setting measurable productivity expectations is a process... and sometimes a long one. Some of my clients struggle for several quarters before they have adequate (not great, not perfect) measures. If you wait until you get it all "right," you may be waiting a very long

time. The process itself, even while you're struggling, adds value as you strive, with your direct reports, to better understand the definition of success for their roles.

**What if I know the right measures but my systems can't track them accurately right now?**
That's okay. This is a process. Don't wait for perfect data. Having a measure that's 75 percent accurate is better than no measure at all. Even having a measure that's 50 percent accurate is a start—and will challenge you to improve it. Don't wait for the perfect dashboard or reporting tool. Numbers written in crayon on the back of a napkin are better than no numbers at all. Start where you are and improve over time.

## Setting Culture Fit Expectations

The second factor is culture fit. Some team members are incredibly productive, but they may also be toxic to the organization. And yet, we call them superstars or A-players without accounting for how they're impacting everyone else's performance and mindset. For balance, we need to measure for culture fit as well as productivity.

Here's a simple way to think about whether a team member is a good culture fit:
*Do they make the people around them better or worse?*
*Are they adding to your desired culture, or subtracting from it?*

### Core Values
An effective way to make culture fit clear, and have a way to measure it, is to create a small number of nonnegotiable core values. *Core values are nonnegotiable behaviors that anchor your culture.* They're not words or phrases that look great on a website. They're not created as a marketing tactic. They're about specific behaviors you hold

team members accountable for. Core values are characteristics that boil up from what's best, what's right, and what's most noble about your culture.

They are behaviors that you communicate, reinforce, and model every day. You also use them in your hiring process to ensure you hire people who live your core values. Core values are not aspirational; they are not behaviors or actions you strive for. They are standards for behaviors and actions you expect everyone in the organization to follow—starting, of course, with you and your leadership team.

Every company has a set of core values. For some, they're unwritten but nevertheless part of the culture. For these companies, values evolve from how the company's leaders and employees habitually act. These unwritten core values are not necessarily what most of us would consider a value. For these companies, one of their unwritten but frequently practiced core values might be "Whoever yells the loudest wins," or "Hide your mistakes so no one notices."

The best companies proactively understand who they are. They take their best characteristics and boil them down to create a set of values that define how they work. Through this, they discover what's best, right, and most noble about who they are.

After they define them, they write them down and come up with stories and examples, so customers, partners, and employees fully understand them. They coach the values, reward those who exemplify the values, and hire based on them.

Some of you may call BS when we talk about core values. For many years, I agreed. In my management consulting career (years before I became a coach), I worked with dozens of companies who spent significant time defining their core values. Some bestselling book or "smart" consultant told them it was important, so they did it. However, years later, it was just a plaque on the wall, with no real meaning to anyone.

In fact, when I introduced the idea of setting core values with the leadership team of one of my first coaching clients, the VP of administration got a big smile on her face. "Wait, we already have core values!"

And with that, she ran out of the room. Two minutes later she came back holding a framed poster listing their six core values.

I took it from her and put it against the wall—core values facing the wall. I then asked the leadership team what their core values were.

"I think collaboration is one... no, maybe it's teamwork."

"Don't we have one about respect? Or I thought we did."

They were the leaders of the organization and didn't know what the core values were!

I eventually put them out of their misery by turning the poster around so they could see them. The first one was "Honesty and Integrity."

I decided to put this core value through the first of three tests (I'll share all these tests shortly).

"Are you willing to fire anyone who repeatedly and blatantly violates this core value?"

I expected a very quick "yes" from the group but got some hesitation and pained looks instead. I looked at the CEO and asked what he was thinking.

"Well, we actually encourage our account managers to *not* share all of the details with our clients when we have a problem with their shipments. We keep it pretty high level because we don't want to worry them if we think we've got the problem under control."

Now, I'm not judging whether this is the right way to communicate with clients. However, if you're actively encouraging someone to not be totally honest, "Honesty and Integrity" is not one of your core values.

### The Three Tests of a Core Value

Before we discuss how to discover your core values, let's review the three tests that determine if something is a bona fide core value or just an empty phrase that sounds good but isn't meaningful.

Here are the three tests:

1. Are you committed to firing someone who blatantly and repeatedly violates a core value? For example, you're a marketing company, and you've determined that creativity is a core value.

**Core values are nonnegotiable behaviors** that anchor your culture.

---

That makes sense; successful marketing requires a degree of creativity, so you'd want to make sure your company is rich in creative minds. But what about the accounts-payable clerk in the finance department of that company? Do you expect creativity from that person? What if they do an impeccable job of paying the company's bills but are not especially creative? Would you fire them for not being creative? If the answer is no, creativity is not one of your core values.

2. Are you willing to take a financial hit to uphold this core value? Let's say one of your company's core values is "respect." You treat everyone like grandma; you respect their knowledge and experience. You would never say anything to a customer or vendor that you wouldn't say to your beloved grandmother. What if your top salesperson doesn't embrace this value? That salesperson is responsible for 35 percent of your revenue, but they treat everyone more like a servant than a grandmother. If your company is willing to put up with that behavior rather than risk 35 percent of its revenue, then respect is not a core value.

3. Is this core value alive in your organization today? If that value is not already embraced and routinely exhibited in your company, then that core value is aspirational. If it's something you hope to be but are not today, then it's not a core value. I know it's tempting to create a core value that defines who you want to be rather than who you are. The problem is that it's impossible for a core value to be both nonnegotiable (see the first two tests of a core value) and aspirational. If it's okay to not live a core value today (if it's aspirational, many won't be living it today), the whole idea of core values becomes, at best, just a plaque on the wall, or at worst, a joke.

### Core Values—Actions to Live By

We'll discuss how to use core values to better assess and strengthen talent throughout the remainder of the book. However, to effectively integrate and live the core values within your organization, consider implementing the following additional strategies:

- Initial and ongoing communication: Clearly define each core value with a precise description and examples, ensuring they are communicated thoroughly at the outset and consistently reinforced over time.

- Integration into hiring processes: Develop interview questions specifically designed to identify candidates who already exhibit your core values, ensuring new hires are aligned from the start.

- Emphasis during onboarding: Use the onboarding process to emphasize the importance of core values, with top executives, such as the CEO, personally conveying their significance to new team members.

- Formal and casual recognition: Recognize team members who exemplify core values in both formal settings, like monthly town hall meetings or company newsletters, and casual interactions like pulling someone aside to tell them they did a great job handling a client issue. Recognition doesn't mean having an "employee of the month" award or a core values award. I've seen most companies try that and fail miserably. Let's face it, if you had an "employee of the month" award, the same three or four team members would win the award every month. By month four to five, you'd start asking, "Who hasn't won the award yet? Who could we give this to?" Don't let that be you.

- Theme-based activities: Dedicate each quarter to focusing on a specific core value, organizing activities, challenges, and learning opportunities that highlight and reinforce that value across the organization.

- Visible reminders: Employ creative, visual reminders like themed merchandise, posters, or even naming conference rooms after core values, but only as a supplement to more substantive activities. Shirts and pens become a joke if you're not actually living these values.

These steps will help ensure that your core values are not just words on a wall but are living, breathing elements of your corporate culture.

## WHAT TO DO NOW

Discover your core values.

There are many ways to discover your company's core values. However, my go-to method is the Mission to Mars exercise described by Jim Collins in the book *Built to Last: Successful Habits of Visionary Companies*, which he coauthored with Jerry I. Porras. This exercise should be done as a group by the leadership team.

Here are the key steps:

1. Each leader on the team picks five team members to be included in a fictitious trip to Mars. The Martians don't speak English, so the mission is to show them through action what's best, right, and noble about your organization. The people you pick should be those who best exemplify what's great about your company.

2. For the five people each leader has selected, the leader must write down one or two characteristics that convinced them to pick this person for the mission. You picked Jim because of Jim's attention to detail. You picked Jill because she's so warm and caring. You picked Ezra because he works his butt off to find answers.

3. The leaders then transfer each characteristic to a sticky note. These notes are put on a flip chart, so all characteristics are visible to the group.

4. A facilitator (typically a coach or the CEO), with the help of the group, organizes the notes into groups of similar ideas. For example, "trustworthy" and "honest" might be grouped together. "Productive" and "efficient" might go together.

5   Once the characteristics are arranged in groups of similar ideas, the group takes each set of characteristics through the three tests mentioned earlier. Most of the characteristics cited are going to fail one of the tests. Other characteristics are going to float to the top and be identified as potential core values.

6   The team then needs to discuss and debate it down to the most important three to six ideas. One person then takes ownership for wordsmithing the values and crafting descriptions and some example stories that bring the core values to life so they can be communicated to the entire organization.

**BURNING QUESTIONS**

**What if I don't have the time or support of the leadership team to complete the exercise to create core values?**
You can use a more basic version of this exercise by following the steps by yourself and use the resulting core values for your team. In time, however, getting the leadership team involved and rolling out core values to the entire organization will be a game changer.

## Quick Review

We're doing the wrong things in how we set expectations for our team members:

- We're not measuring the right things
- We're not holding people accountable for those measures
- We're believing performance equals productivity
- We're allowing these unclear expectations to lead to unacceptable results

Introducing the Talent Density Expectations Model. Use these principles to guide the setting of productivity expectations:

- Define a small number of metrics
- Ensure that each metric has a target
- Use higher-frequency measures for best results
- Use both lagging and leading metrics
- "Balance" your metrics
- "Weight" your metrics
- Set expectations collaboratively
- Define role success that drives company success
- Set targets that are achievable, yet realistically high
- Focus on the role, not the person
- Review productivity expectations periodically

Use core values to drive your culture fit expectations. Core values are nonnegotiable behaviors that anchor your culture. The three tests of a core value are:

- Is violating it a fireable offense?
- Are you willing to take a financial hit to uphold the core value?
- Is it alive in the organization today?

Ways to keep your core values "alive" include:

- Initial and ongoing communication
- Integration into hiring processes
- Emphasis during onboarding
- Formal and casual recognition
- Theme-based activities
- Visible reminders

Go to my website strengthoftalent.com to access my book resources, where you'll find these helpful tools:

- A worksheet you can use to complete the Functional Accountability Chart
- Sample productivity measures by organizational function (sales, marketing, finance, etc.) and a template to help you work through productivity expectations for each of your direct reports
- Sample core values and a set of activities to ensure your team and company are living and breathing those core values

To help set and track these expectations, go to talentdensitysystems.com to learn about this system and claim your free three-month access to the tool.

**STEP 2**

# ASSESS PERFORMANCE

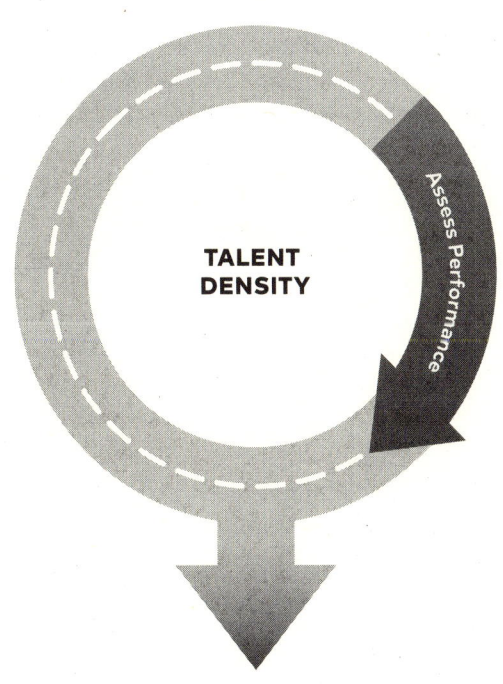

## Assessing Performance—the Wrong Way

We're assessing performance the wrong way. Or worse, not assessing it at all.

We all assess performance in our heads...

"Why can't he just do it right the first time!"

"Thank goodness I have her on the team to make my life easier!"

But are those assessments accurate? Even if they are, most of us keep those assessments in our heads until the problem is so big we have no choice.

Here are some key mistakes we're regularly making:

### We're Too Subjective

"I know good performance when I see it." Really?

"Just do your best." What does that mean?

"I need you to be more productive." Does that just mean work faster?

We've already discussed the importance of setting clear expectations in Step 1. Without clear expectations, an effective assessment of performance is almost impossible. Without clear expectations, our team members are frustrated and confused. Without clear expectations, any assessment of performance includes too many surprises.

### We Do It Too Infrequently

The ugly truth is, many of our team members have no idea how they're doing. The low-performing team members think they're doing okay, and as a result, they keep plugging along, hurting the team. And the high-performing team members aren't aware they're exceeding our expectations and, as a result, never feel like they're "winning," causing them to leave for a better opportunity or burn out.

For far too many leaders, assessing the performance of their direct reports is an afterthought and takes a back seat to more urgent (but not more important) activities. Assessing performance is critically important but will never be more urgent than a client fire drill or fixing the mess created by a low-performing team member. We need to prioritize the important and the urgent or the cycle will continue. We can't wait until an emergency or an annual performance review to dive deep into how our team members are doing against expectations.

### We're Not Having Enough Discussions and Debates

As leaders, we typically assess talent behind closed doors. "Get your performance reviews done and send them to HR for review and filing." This process assumes we're "all knowing" about our team members performance. We're *not!!*

Many of our peers interact with our direct reports as well. Discussing and debating your assessment with your peers will give you a much fuller story of their performance. You may not see how they're interacting with other teams, but your peers do. You may believe one of your direct reports is living your core values at the highest level... because they're always on their best behavior with you. Your peers can help open your eyes to behaviors you never see or can reinforce what you already know from your experience.

Your peers will also add tremendous value in helping you determine the most effective actions to take to increase strength of talent on your team (more on that in Step 3) and plant the seed for additional accountability (more on that in Step 4).

### We Don't Focus Enough on Culture Fit

As discussed in Step 1, performance does not equal productivity. Performance is a combination of both productivity and culture fit. Many organizations place a high value on assessing productivity but low or no value on assessing culture fit. Not only is this a problem, but I'd argue that culture fit is even more important than productivity. Productivity can be coached, but nine times out of ten, culture fit cannot. More on this in Step 3.

### We Misuse "Potential"

"I know she hasn't hit her goals in the last three quarters, but I'll keep coaching her because she has potential."

I'm a fan of potential and I believe everyone has it. Our most important job as leaders is to help our people maximize their potential. However, many leaders use "potential" as an excuse to tolerate low performance.

At the end of the day, our companies run on productivity and our work environment is built on culture fit. Potential doesn't solve either of these.

As leaders, we need to use the idea of potential to motivate us to coach, develop, and challenge our people. Sometimes, we need to make the tough decision if someone, despite their potential, isn't suited for their current role... or for the company overall.

If we use potential as an excuse to delay difficult decisions or conversations, we're suboptimizing our company's performance. We're also hurting that team member who may have greater opportunity to be a higher performer in another role, or somewhere else.

### The Right Way: The Talent Assessment Model

Now that we've set both culture fit and productivity expectations, we need a process to assess performance against these expectations.

Enter the Talent Assessment Model.

### Purpose of the Model

The purpose of this model is to enable productive conversations about strengthening the talent within your organization. It creates a common language across leaders on how talent is assessed, the actions that are required to develop that talent, and making the tough decision to transition someone out of the organization who's not a strong fit. This model and the associated assessment categories drive debate, action, and accountability at a level not feasible using traditional performance management frameworks.

**Debate:** The use of a common language for setting expectations and categorizing performance drives fact-based discussions among leaders. As you progress through this book, I'll describe when those discussions happen and how they drive more thorough and accurate assessments of performance.

**Action:** As you'll see in Step 3, categorizing performance using this model drives the identification of more specific and more powerful actions to strengthen talent in each of the four levels of performance.

**Accountability:** The model also allows each leader to better assess whether their actions are having the desired effect on their direct reports and the team. As you'll see in Step 4, this leads to improved accountability as leaders are more able to hold themselves, and their teams, accountable for strengthening team talent by using a specific measure called the Talent Density Indicator.

The model helps assess team members against expectations, *not* force-rank them. Please don't mistake this for the stories we've all heard about the General Electric days under Jack Welch where the bottom 10 percent of people were fired every year. In this model, it's absolutely possible for all team members to be performing at a high level. It's also possible for everyone to be performing at a low level. It's not about comparing people to one another; it's about comparing their actual performance to agreed expectations.

**The more frequently you assess talent,** the more frequently you can develop talent.

---

The purpose of this model is not only to assess your direct reports. It's also to assess how well you're leading them, inspiring them, coaching them, and making tough decisions on low-performing team members. If one of your team members fails, you've failed. We too often focus on the fact that we might have hired the wrong person, when the reality is we can do a better job helping them become the right person.

Lastly, the purpose of this model is *not* to share these ratings with your direct reports. Telling a direct report which performance category they're in results in defensiveness, not productive conversation. A low-to-medium-performing team member's first reaction to being given a rating is to become upset and/or argue for why they deserve a better rating. Neither of those reactions is conducive to a constructive conversation. Even giving someone a strong rating can be detrimental to constructive conversation if it causes them to be complacent. Share your feedback and discuss actions. *Do not share their specific rating.*

### Frequency of the Assessment

While you must always be assessing direct report performance, this more formal assessment takes place quarterly, at the very least. Steps 3, 4, and 5 in the process (which are the next three chapters of this book) occur quarterly as well.

This is *not* a once-per-year activity.

*The more frequently you assess talent, the more frequently you can develop talent.*

### How It Works

As you can see, the Talent Assessment Model has two axes, productivity and culture fit. Each is scored from 0 (low performing) to 10 (high performing).

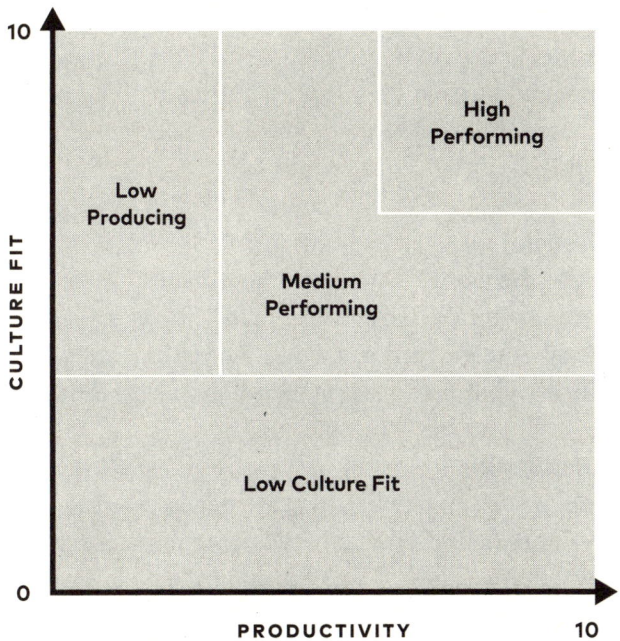

The resulting performance categories are as follows:

**High Performing**
A team member is performing at a high level only if they score high in both culture fit and productivity—the upper right category of the model. I'll discuss the specifics of which scores I consider "high" and which are "low" shortly.

**Low Culture Fit**
Notice the horizontal line going all the way across the model. Team members that are a poor culture fit are toxic to your organization. Does that mean they're bad people? No. It just means they're a bad fit for your organization.

The culture fit line goes all the way across, which indicates it doesn't matter how productive they are; if they're not living the core values, they are toxic to your organization. That can be a difficult concept for leaders to internalize. How can a salesperson closing the most deals be toxic to our organization? But we know if someone isn't living our nonnegotiable core values, they're hurting our culture and hurting the morale and productivity of everyone around them. That's toxic no matter how much revenue they're bringing in.

**Low Producing**

Notice I use the word "producing" here instead of "performing." That's because this performance category focuses specifically on productivity. A team member who's living the core values at an acceptable level but producing at a low level is low producing.

**Medium Performing**

Everyone else—team members that are not assessed at a high level for both culture fit and productivity but are not at the low producing or low culture fit level—is performing at a medium level.

## Completing the Assessment

The problem with most talent assessment frameworks is they're too subjective. They don't take into account that some leaders are hard graders and some are easy. This not only makes the assessment less valuable, it also hurts our ability to hold our leaders accountable for specific talent development activities. If a leader is an easy grader—"Everyone's doing great!"—there's little to hold them accountable for driving their team to greater results. If a leader is a hard scorer, you have the opposite problem that "everyone needs to get better at everything." Subjective frameworks also tend to focus on whether a leader likes that person, not whether they're truly performing. This hurts the company, and it hurts the team member who's not getting the coaching and development they need to realize their potential.

To make this more objective, create specific guidelines for both productivity and culture fit. Guidelines may not be perfect, but having them dramatically increases the accuracy of the assessment.

The power of having specific measures for productivity and culture fit is that it gives us a common language that allows a common understanding and injects more precision and objectivity into our assessment. It lessens the gap between the easy graders and the hard graders. And remember, these guidelines should be used in tandem with the productivity and culture fit expectations you set in Step 1.

My recommended guidelines are illustrated in the Productivity and Culture Fit Guidelines tables.

| Productivity Guidelines | |
|---|---|
| Score | Description |
| 10 | Goes above and beyond, exceeding all goals and metrics |
| 9 | Achieves at least 90% of all goals and metrics |
| 8 | Achieves 80–89% of goals and metrics |
| 7 | Achieves 70–79% of goals and metrics |
| 6 | Achieves 60–69% of goals and metrics |
| 5 | Achieves 50–59% of goals and metrics |
| 4 | Achieves 40–49% of goals and metrics |
| 3 | Achieves 30–39% of goals and metrics |
| 2 | Achieves 20–29% of goals and metrics |
| 1 | Achieves 10–19% of goals and metrics |
| 0 | Achieves less than 10% of goals and metrics |

| Culture Fit Guidelines | |
|---|---|
| Score | Description |
| 10 | Lives our core values at a high level and is a model for the rest of the organization |
| 9 | Lives all core values consistently |
| 8 | Lives our core values consistently but occasionally has challenges with one or two of them |
| 7 | Has frequent challenges with one or two core values |
| 6 | Has frequent challenges with more than two core values |
| 5 | Has frequent challenges with several core values and has a large negative impact on others |
| 4 | Blatantly and repeatedly violates several core values and is significantly impacting the work environment |
| 3 or below | Why are they still here? |

For productivity, someone is a 10 out of 10 only if they're blowing away their goals. Not just meeting expectations but creating new ones. At a 9, they're achieving at least 90 percent of all of their goals, and it goes down the list. Remember, when calculating the productivity score, use the weighting we discussed in the "Setting Productivity Expectations" section in Step 1.

For culture fit, we need to take something that on the surface seems very subjective and inject some objectivity. We can do that by using our nonnegotiable core values that I described in Step 1. Again, someone is not a 10 out of 10 if they're simply living the core values. They're a 10 out of 10 if they're living them all at such a high level that they're a model for the rest of the organization. The Serena Williams, Michael Jordan, or Simone Biles of core values. A 9 is they're living the core values. An 8 is they're occasionally having trouble with one or two. A 7 means they're frequently having trouble with one or two core values... and on down the list.

Let's review how those guidelines map to the Talent Assessment Model.

**High Performing:** I recommend putting an 8.5 in the boxes next to the horizontal and vertical lines around the "High" square in the Talent Assessment Model. That means that to be a high performer, you must score 9 or higher in both core values and productivity. Notice I always end my numbers with ".5," as this forces people into the categories (high performing, medium performing, low producing, low culture fit) without anyone being on the line.

**Low Culture Fit:** How low does a culture fit score have to be to make someone a low culture fit? I recommend using 7.5 (again, use a fraction so no one falls on the line). That means anyone who scores 7 or below in culture fit is determined to be a low culture fit. I know that sounds harsh, but remember, your core values are nonnegotiable behaviors. Scoring a 7 out of 10 on nonnegotiable behaviors should be unacceptable.

**Low Producing:** The next piece of the puzzle is the rectangle on the mid to upper left. These are folks who may be embodying your core values, but their productivity is so low that they are hurting the company. They may be wonderful people who fit in well, but they are not productive. I recommend putting 6.5 in that box (again, use a fraction so no one falls on the line). That means anyone who scores a 6 or below in productivity is determined to be performing at a "low productivity" level, unless they've already been assessed as a "low culture fit."

**Medium Performing:** Anyone not fitting any of the other categories are your medium-performing team members, who score high enough to not be low producing or a low culture fit but don't score high enough to be a high performer.

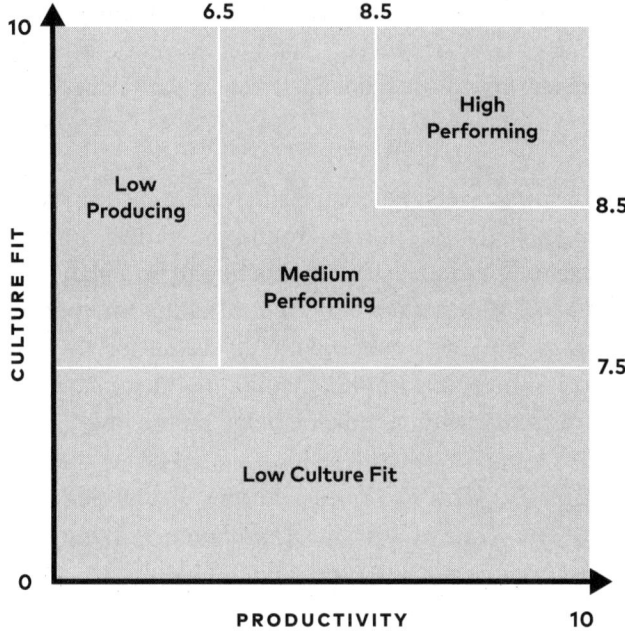

It's at this point that many leaders begin to make excuses for their direct reports.

"I know he's missing his sales targets, but it's not his fault. We just implemented a new sales strategy, and it may take a quarter or two to show benefits."

"I know she hasn't been living our 'We lift each other up' core value, but we haven't done a good job, as a company, communicating our values to the organization."

"I know he hasn't hit his client retention goal, but I haven't had the time to coach him on it."

These all may be valid points. However, remember the purpose of this process is *not* to label team member performance for the purpose of calculating raises or promotions. It's *not* so it goes in their "permanent record" and follows them forever. The purpose *is* to help determine appropriate actions to strengthen the talent of your team (more on this in Step 3). The purpose *is* for leaders to be able to hold each other accountable for improving the performance of each member of their team (more on this in Step 4). If we inflate our assessments, we'll miss key actions that drive growth and our ability to hold each other accountable for taking those actions. We'll end up in a situation where the VP of sales will have all "high performers" and yet be missing most sales targets. The director of customer service will have all "high performers" and yet client retention may be falling drastically.

A person's performance against expectations is not only based on their activity. It's based on how the company is doing, how their leader is leading them, and outside factors like the economy, competition, regulation, etc. The actions and accountability that follow the assessment should reflect that.

Let's look at those excuses again with appropriate actions...

"I know he's missing his sales targets, but it's not his fault. We just implemented a new sales strategy, and it may take a quarter or two to show benefits."

**Action:** Continue to coach on the new sales strategy and continue to tweak that strategy until sales increase.

"I know she hasn't been living our 'We lift each other up' core value, but we haven't done a good job, as a company, communicating our values to the organization."

**Action:** As a company, execute a plan to further educate the organization on the core values. As an individual leader, don't wait for the company to do something. Improve your team's understanding of the core values right now.

"I know he hasn't hit his client retention goal, but I haven't had the time to coach him on it."

**Action:** Make the time! Coach, train, strategize... do whatever it takes to help your direct report hit the target.

To take this a step further, if most of your team members are performing at a low level, that may be a clue that *they're* not the problem. The problem may be *you!*

We'll revisit assessments again during the quarterly talent assessment meeting (QTAM) in Step 4, where your peers will get a chance to question, challenge, and debate your assessment. Very often, there are situations and behaviors they and their teams see that you don't.

---

**WHAT TO DO NOW**

**Assess yourself:**
Use the expectations you set (both productivity and culture fit) in Step 1, to assess your own performance.

1. Use the Productivity Guidelines to give yourself a score between 1 and 10 on productivity.
2. Use the Culture Fit Guidelines to give yourself a score between 1 and 10 on culture fit.
3. Determine which performance category you're in by using the Talent Assessment Model.
4. Determine what actions you can take to improve your performance. Additional actions for each level of performance will be covered in Step 3, but do your best now.

**Assess your team:**
Use the expectations you set (both productivity and culture fit) in Step 1 to assess each of your direct reports. For each direct report, follow these steps:

1. Use the Productivity Guidelines to give each a score between 1 and 10 on productivity.
2. Use the Culture Fit Guidelines to give each a score between 1 and 10 on culture fit.
3. Determine which performance category each is in by using the Talent Assessment Model.

4. Determine what actions you can take to improve each direct report's performance. Additional actions for each level of performance will be covered in Step 3, but do your best now.

## BURNING QUESTIONS

**Can you really represent the entirety of someone's performance with a couple of numbers?**
No, but we can use numbers to dramatically improve the way most leaders assess performance today. Using these metrics helps inject more facts, accuracy, and objectivity into a process that just doesn't work well today.

**What if I haven't yet been able to identify the right productivity expectations for one of my direct reports? Should I not assess them until I do?**
This is a common challenge. It's not always easy to come up with the right metrics, and perfection is not required. Do the best you can and tweak them over time. If you truly have no metrics to use, do your best to assess productivity anyway on the 1 to 10 scale. This may be "winging" it a bit, but if you define productivity by their results, and not how long and hard they're working, your estimate will probably be not that far off.

**What if a team member's low productivity score is not their fault? What if it's due to overall poor company performance or a bad economy?**
Regardless of the reason, a team members productivity should be measured against their targets. That doesn't always mean it's their fault. After all, this process is not about placing blame; it's about identifying corrective action. By highlighting the low productivity, it will challenge us, as leaders, to brainstorm actions. Sometimes these actions go beyond coaching or developing an individual team member. They might include changes to company strategy, team dynamics, leadership tactics, or other steps outside of the control of one team member.

**Why not a more detailed 10 x 10 gradient? Wouldn't that be more accurate than the four categories in the Talent Density Model?**
The purpose for this process is coming up with actions and holding leaders accountable, not grading team members at the most detailed level and then giving them their grades. A 10 x 10 scale is just too much detail, without adding real value. The more categories you have, the more time you'll spend agonizing over which category they fit in. And the more time your peers will spend challenging you on that category (more on peer involvement in the process in Step 4). That precious time is better spent determining the right actions to take to improve the strength of talent and executing those actions, not debating details that don't add value.

**What if I have no core values? How do I score culture fit?**
There are three recommendations: First, if you don't have a set of non-negotiable core values in your organization, I recommend making it a priority to discover them. Second, just because you don't have an agreed-upon set of company core values, doesn't mean you don't know them when you see them. Do your best, as an individual leader, to identify three to six nonnegotiable behaviors for your team, and use those as a substitute. Third, if the first two ideas don't work for you, do your best to assess culture fit on a 1 to 10 scale anyway. An easy way to look at it is by asking, "Are they making the people around them better or worse? Are they adding to, or subtracting from, your desired culture?"

## Labels

Before we go any further, let's talk about labels.

The language we use to label how someone is performing is critical because it impacts how we think about the person and, therefore, what actions we take.

In my last book, *Breakthrough Leadership Team*, and in my work with clients for many years, I used the terms "A-player," "B-player," "C-player," and "Toxic C-player." Notice I now use the terms "High Performing," "Medium Performing," "Low Producing," and "Low Culture Fit."

That seems like a minor distinction, but it's not.

I learned this a few years ago while working with a new client. The leadership team and I were discussing potential actions for several team members who the leadership team and I called B-players. What I heard made me cringe, and it was my fault. They were talking about these people as if that's just who they were: "You know B-players, they just want to do enough not to get fired." "They're all about going home at 5 p.m. whether the job is done or not." "You can't trust these people to work from home. If we can't see them, they're probably only working about 50 percent of the time."

It was as if thirty-five years ago, their mother had given birth to an eight-pound, two-ounce B-player. Of course it doesn't work that way.

Hearing enough, I finally said, "Is it possible these folks are performing at that level because of you? Is it possible you're not challenging them enough? Not spending enough time coaching them? Is it possible you haven't been clear enough on your vision for the company and the role they play in getting there?"

*It's not who they are; it's how they're performing.*

The leadership team needed to take responsibility, and by calling people B-players, they got off easy. There's not much a leader can do for someone who's just a B-player. It's the B-player's fault.

Here's a quick grammar lesson to understand the difference. The word "player" is a noun, and a noun describes a person, place, or thing. By calling someone an A-Player, B-Player, or C-Player, we're describing who they are. Psychologically, that instills more of a static mindset. If that's who they are, what can I do? I guess I just hired the wrong person and need to try again. The words "performing" or "producing" are verbs. A verb describes an action, state, or occurrence. It's what they're currently doing, not who they are.

**"Potential" is an excuse we make** for people who aren't performing yet.

Using a verb instills more of a growth mindset. One where we can clearly imagine the person taking a different set of actions. One where we might be able to help them take those actions.

Even folks performing at the highest level should not be called A-players. Although it sounds like a compliment, it's not a useful way to think about them. If I call someone an A-player, it sounds like that's just who they are. I can leave them alone and go focus on my low-performing team members. That's exactly how to *not* treat people that are performing at a high level. You should be spending most of your time with them. They're the people you can best leverage to reach your team or company goals. They're the people who want to be challenged. And they're the people on the phone right now with a recruiter who's offering them 50 percent more to go work for your competition.

I also want to explain why I changed the term "Toxic-C" to "Low Culture Fit." While I absolutely believe that having someone on your team who is not living your core values is toxic to the team, too many leaders shy away from calling someone "toxic." I get it. Someone not living your core values is not a bad person. They're just a bad fit for your team. Calling someone toxic can be interpreted as too "judgy." Too much like you're calling them a bad person. This causes some leaders to overstate a team member's culture fit score, so they don't have to label them toxic. I've found that calling it Low Culture Fit has less of a stigma and, therefore, the culture fit score becomes more accurate and honest. Also notice that Low Culture Fit is not a verb like High-Performing, Medium-Performing or Low-Producing. That's also purposeful. Remember, I changed the other labels to verbs because it's what they're currently doing—it's not who they are. For someone not living your core values, more than likely it *is* who they are, which means they may not be coachable. More on that in Step 3.

Therefore, please be careful with labels. If you find yourself or your team using terms like A-player, B-player, C-player or Toxic C-player, stop and use the more useful terms in the Talent Assessment Model instead.

## Quick Review

We're doing the wrong things in assessing the performance of our team members:

- We're too subjective.
- We do it too infrequently.
- We don't drive enough discussion and debate.
- We don't focus enough on culture fit.
- We misuse "potential."

Introducing the Talent Assessment Model:

### Purpose
- To enable productive conversations about strengthening the talent within your organization
- To drive debate, action, and accountability

### Frequency
- Formally: Quarterly
- Informally: All the time

### The Categories of Performance
- High Performing
- Medium Performing
- Low Producing
- Low Culture Fit

We need to be careful with labels and the difference between who someone is and how they're performing.

Go to my website strengthoftalent.com to access my book resources for a self-assessment and direct reports assessment worksheet.

To automate and improve the accuracy of your assessment, go to talentdensitysystems.com to learn about this system and claim your free three-month access to the tool.

STEP 3

# ACT

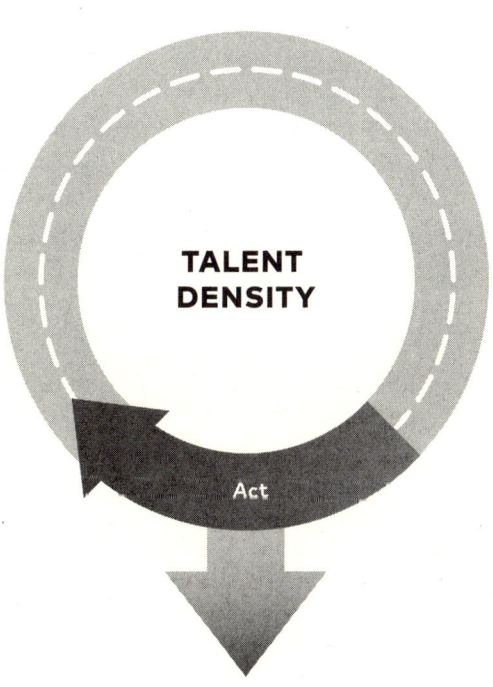

### Act—the Wrong Way

When we don't adequately set expectations or assess performance, we can't focus on taking the right actions with and for our team members. Therefore, we take the wrong actions or take no action at all.

Here are some key mistakes we're regularly making:

#### We Don't Prioritize "Taking Action" on Team Member Performance

Ramon is in his backyard trying to saw a log in half. He's been out there for hours. His neighbor Miguel sees him laboring and says, "Ramon, you've been out here forever. Check your blade—it probably needs sharpening. Let's go to my shed and I can sharpen that for you." Ramon responds, "No thanks, Miguel, I don't have the time. I've got to saw this log in half."

Not prioritizing taking action on team member performance means we're working with a dull blade.

Developing people tends to be an afterthought after you get your "important" work done. Since the "important" work is never done, the "people" work doesn't happen.

#### We Don't Know How to Effectively Impact Performance

Because they don't effectively prioritize taking action on team member performance, many leaders don't understand the different tools in their toolbox to impact performance. While they might get some training on how to motivate people in a Leadership 101 course, they don't understand and practice the nuances of coaching, giving feedback, or holding people accountable. Leaders may not have the skill set or tools for helping team members move up and to the right on the Talent Assessment Model.

### We Put Too Much Onus on Whether We Hired Right or Not

Having a thorough and effective hiring process is key. Anything you can do to improve that process is well worth the investment. When a team member is underperforming, I've seen leaders lay almost all the blame on the hiring process and very little on how we've coached and developed that team member since they've been hired. We like to talk about developing our people, but some leaders have more of a static mindset: "I've either hired right or hired wrong." It's not that simple.

### We Overinvest in Low-Performing Team Members

I recently facilitated a workshop with fifteen CEOs and got into a discussion about the time they were investing in their high- versus low-performing team members.

At one point, I was challenged by one CEO who said, "Let's be real, if I've got these low performers, and if I don't spend more time with them, they're going to cause more problems."

I responded, "If you're spending too much time with low performers, then you've got too many low performers."

If you feel like you can't spend enough time with your highest performers, because you're dealing with the impacts of your low performers, you have not taken effective action. You haven't taken enough time to either coach them to an acceptable level of performance or coach them out of your organization.

Here's another way to think about it... how often does working on a weakness, an area where we may not have natural talent, turn that weakness into a strength? There's a much higher probability that we'll just get to an acceptable, mediocre level. And how do we *feel* when we're working in an area where we have no natural talent? Stressed, frustrated?

I've seen people work hard on their weaknesses... and all they got was tired.

So, if we're stressed, frustrated, tired, *and* not spending much time working on our strengths, what happens to those strengths? They get stale. Weaker strengths and stronger weaknesses don't make us great... or happy. They make us mediocre.

Now think about that at a team level.

Will we get the most benefit trying to fix our low performers, our weaknesses, or leveraging and developing our highest performers, our strengths?

By spending most of our time with our low performers, we wind up with a mediocre team. Our low performers may see some improvement but we're not leveraging, developing, and retaining our *best* people!

Spending most of your time with your high performers gives you your *greatest ROI* and your *greatest chance* of creating an extraordinary team.

### We Don't Have the Difficult Conversations or Make the Difficult Decisions

Too many leaders shy away from having difficult conversations. They'd rather sweep a problem under the rug than have the uncomfortable feelings that come with confronting someone about the level at which they're producing or the behaviors they're exhibiting.

Difficult discussion or not, we sometimes need to make difficult decisions regarding a team member's fit for their role or fit for our organization. I've seen too many leaders delay those decisions too long or never make them at all... hurting their company, their team, themselves, *and* the low-performing team member.

### We Make Decisions Based on the Perceived Immaturity of Our People

I was working with a client recently who wanted to share detailed cost and profitability information with their direct reports. When this idea came up, two other leaders expressed concern. They feared some team members couldn't handle the information. They might misinterpret the numbers or share them outside the organization.

As a result, they were about to put a stop to sharing the information because they perceived that some people in the organization were not mature enough to handle it. They were about to stifle the growth of these individuals and the company.

Have you underestimated your team's maturity and ability to handle information? And, therefore, made decisions based on the perceived immaturity of your people?

Avoid decisions based on your lowest-performing team members. Optimize decisions and actions for your highest performers.

Trust that your teams can handle the truth.

If you've hired, coached, and developed them, you should assume they have the maturity to deal with important information and decisions.

Otherwise, you risk "dumbing down" your organization, making it impossible to achieve your most exciting goals and visions.

## The Right Way: Prioritizing Action

Without action, the Talent Assessment Model is a waste of time. There's little point in setting expectations or assessing performance without a commitment to taking massive action to improve strength of talent on our teams. That's why this is the most critical and longest step in the book.

Before diving into specific actions I recommend for each level of performance, it's important to understand some key philosophies that guide these actions.

### The #1 Driver of Profit Growth Is People Growth

This is the driving philosophy of this entire book, so it cannot be restated enough. Every leader's top priority should be to strengthen the talent of their team. A great strategy with a mediocre team will fail. A great team with a mediocre strategy will ultimately succeed as they learn fast and change the strategy.

## If You Want a Great Company, You Need a Great Team

This may sound obvious, but sometimes inertia takes over. It's easy to stick with the team you've got and do the best you can. Making changes (changing people's roles or transitioning out team members not performing) is never easy. But here's the truth: If you wouldn't enthusiastically rehire everyone on your team, you don't have the right team.

## Everyone Can Be High Performing... Somewhere

Many years ago, I owned a staffing and recruiting firm. I had a woman working for me as a staffing supervisor. That job required meticulous attention to detail, crossing all the t's and dotting the i's.

The problem was, she was the most scattered person I had ever worked with. She struggled with details and wasn't performing well in the role.

On the other hand, she had the incredible ability to walk into a room of fifty strangers and leave with thirty new best friends. She relished talking to angry, unhappy clients and had a natural talent for relationship-building.

But in her current role, she was ineffective, so she and I had to have a very difficult conversation.

I told her that while she was incredibly talented in certain ways, she didn't exhibit the skills to succeed in the role I needed her to fill. However, I was confident that if she found a role better suited to her talents, she'd be a superstar.

While she wasn't thrilled about being fired, she eventually found a sales role in another organization and had amazing success there.

When we keep underperformers around out of misplaced loyalty, we're hurting ourselves, our company, and them.

Everyone has talents, but they may not be the talents you need within your organization right now. Everyone has skills, but they may not have the skills they need to perform at an elite level within your organization.

Keeping them around, underperforming or performing at a mediocre level, is not only hurting your organization, but also keeping them unproductive and unfulfilled.

Sometimes being loyal to them means having that difficult conversation and motivating them to find a place where they can excel.

Maybe that's within your company, which means coaching, developing them, challenging them, or redefining their role so they transform from underperforming to superstar.

Or maybe it's helping them see that their best opportunities lie outside your company.

I want to challenge you as a leader to take the responsibility of helping *everyone* on your team become a high performer, whether that's inside or outside of your organization.

**Fire Fast, Hire Slow**

Most companies do the opposite.

Remember the first story in this book about the CEO that waited much too long to fire his low-performing CFO? He fired slow and hired fast.

Now, hiring slow does *not* mean dragging your feet and taking your time. It means ensuring you have a thorough recruiting, screening, evaluating, and hiring process. A hiring mistake is one of the biggest, most expensive mistakes we can make. While the focus of this book is *not* on the hiring process, the best hiring methodology I know of is Topgrading. Read *Who: The A Method for Hiring* by Geoff Smart and Randy Street to learn more.

And remember, firing fast is *not* heartless. If everyone can be a high performer somewhere, sometimes letting people go is the most loving thing we can do for them.

**Overinvest in High-Performing Team Members**

Most leaders overinvest in low performers and underinvest in high performers. "Thank God I don't need to worry about her (a high-performing team member), so I can go take care of my problem folks (low-performing team members)."

As a leader, you should be spending most of your time with your best people! They're the folks who you can leverage to be great. They're the folks who can attract other great people. They're the folks with the most potential.

**The more time you spend developing your best people,** the less time you'll spend frustrated with your results.

———————————

Recall the 1 = 3 philosophy from earlier in the book, where one superstar equals the productivity of three average performers. There is no greater return on investment than the investment you make in your high-performing team members.

Here's another way to look at it using simple math: The impact of improving the performance of a high performer by 10 percent is *much* greater than the impact of improving a low performer's performance by 10 percent. For that reason, the more time you spend developing your best people, the less time you'll spend frustrated with your results.

## Maybe You Didn't Hire Wrong, You're Just Not Leading Right

It's too easy to believe that an underperforming team member was just a bad hire. While, of course, there are instances where bad hiring decisions lead to underperformance, our leadership is the problem much more often than we'd like to believe. Are you taking consistent, powerful action to inspire them, teach them, coach them, hold them accountable, and challenge them? Are you setting high standards, modeling those standards, and accepting nothing less? When confronting low or medium performance, look in the mirror first.

I've organized the rest of Step 3 in a way I think will help you make the decisions required to take massive action to increase your team's strength of talent.

First, I'll guide you through recommended actions specific to each category of performance (high performing, medium performing, low producing and low culture fit).

Second, I'll detail my recommendations for improving overall team performance. Most of these ideas are actions that will have a positive impact on the team, regardless of how they're currently performing.

Third, I'll share my framework for regular one-on-one meetings with each of your direct reports. One-on-one meetings are typically neglected ("I don't have the time for all these meetings!"), often mismanaged, and very often are the critical missing link to a high-performing team.

Last, I'll help you better tackle difficult conversations. These are critical conversations we tend to screw up or shy away from, but that can make an incredible difference to our company and the lives of our team members.

## Actions for High-Performing Team Members

When I ask my clients where we need to take the highest-priority actions, which team members we need to focus on first—high performing, medium performing, or low performing—most want to focus on the low-performing folks. "Let's fix our big problems first." This is exactly the wrong thing to do.

High-performing team members have the biggest potential for growth. I know it sounds counterintuitive, but while they may be performing at a high level now, they're probably capable of much more. In addition to their potential for growth, these are the folks who are most likely to leave your organization out of boredom because they're not being challenged, or because they get a better job opportunity somewhere else. High-performing team members are typically the formal or informal leaders of your organization. If they are driving toward results, if they are passionate about what they're doing, if they are increasing their performance, that cascades down to the rest of the organization. And lastly, superstars tend to know other superstars, so you need to ensure your high-performing team members feel great about referring other potential high performers.

Early in my career, I always had the hardest time writing performance reviews for my best people. For low performers, it was easy to convey clear areas of improvement and advise on how to improve performance. But, for my high performers, I was at a loss. "They're already doing great—how can I add value?" "They're smarter than me—how can I help them?"

*If they don't grow with you, they'll grow with someone else.*

Let's dive into some specific actions you should be thinking about (and acting on!) with and for your high-performing team

**If they don't grow with you,** they'll grow with someone else.

———————

members. While this is not an exhaustive list (you will certainly come up with additional ideas), it's a great start.

1. **Challenge them.** Challenge your high-performing team members to learn something new or do something new. Take a difficult challenge you're dealing with and assign it to them.

2. **Raise the bar.** If they're consistently meeting or beating their productivity expectations, set a higher standard. Challenge them to get creative to reach higher targets. No need to be dictatorial here. Let them know what a great job they're doing and ask for their help as to where they think they can raise the bar.

3. **Increase their responsibility.** What additional functions or tasks can you give them responsibility for? Where are you overwhelmed or stretched too thin? Maybe they can jump in and grab accountability from you. High-performing team members love adding additional accountabilities—if they're not stretched too thin themselves, and if they know these additional tasks and skills will help them progress in their career.

4. **Invest in them.** Where do they need to improve their skills, build their network, or gain more industry exposure? Invest additional time or dollars by sending them to a conference, allowing them to take a training course or hire a coach. Your ROI (and theirs) will be well worth it.

5. **Promote them.** Is there an opportunity to promote them? This may simply be a change in title or come with additional responsibilities.

6. **Ask them to mentor or coach someone else.** Is there a new member of your team who requires some mentoring? Is there a team member struggling to perform? Ask your high-performing team member to help. It'll boost their confidence and feeling of accomplishment. You'll improve the performance of other team members. And you'll get a sense for their potential as a leader.

7. **Reward them.** How can you better reward them for a job well done? This may be monetary, in the form of a salary increase or bonus, or nonmonetary, in the form of flexible scheduling, additional time off, or a dinner out with their family.

8. **Recognize them.** Recognition can be a big public shout-out—for example, at your next monthly company town hall: "I just want to thank Caitlin for doing such an amazing job managing our CRM implementation. Let's give her a round of applause." Or it may just be an informal, verbal pat on the back.

9. **Remove barriers.** Is a clunky process getting in their way? Fix it! Are low performers hurting their ability to move forward? Take care of it! Are you micromanaging? Get out of their way!

10. **Give them more exposure.** This exposure could be more industry exposure, client exposure, or internal company exposure. An example of company exposure, if they're not on the leadership team, could be inviting them to the leadership team's weekly meeting to present something: "Alex, you did such an amazing job implementing our new product development process, I'd love for you to come share it with the leadership team in our next weekly meeting." This is exciting, and an honor. They're going home and telling their spouse, kids, dog, or anyone that will listen.

11. **Conduct an accelerator session.** I learned this from my good friend Keith Cupp of Gravitas Impact Premium Coaches. It's a session that can be constructed to include all high-potential leaders of your organization. In this facilitated session the group discusses, debates, and collaborates on topics important to the company. The results of these discussions are then presented back to the leadership team. This adds great value to the company and helps the leadership team identify the next candidates to sit around the executive leadership team table. Specific discussions can include (but are not limited to) the following questions:

- What are the company's most important strengths, weaknesses, opportunities, and threats (SWOT analysis)?
- What should the company start doing, stop doing, or keep doing?
- How can the company better live our core values?
- What should the top company priorities be for the next year?

12 **Create a Mars Team.** You might remember the Mission to Mars exercise to discover your core values, from Step 1. Several years ago, one of my clients came up with an ingenious idea: Why not ask the folks you decided to send to Mars (the team members who best model your core values) to become part of a team that focuses on company culture? Up to a certain level of investment, this group has the permission to implement anything they believe will help the company better live its core values. Ideas they came up with included creating a video where team members told stories and thanked other team members for living a specific core value, putting the core values on the steps leading up to the office, and coming up with questions to ask on interviews to determine if a job candidate was already living those core values.

13 **Help them join a mastermind.** In his 1937 book, *Think and Grow Rich*, Napoleon Hill discussed the idea of the Master Mind, which referred to two or more people coming together in harmony to solve problems. There are many mastermind groups available to CEOs. Groups like Vistage International, TEC Canada, Young Presidents' Organization, and Women Presidents Organization are all great examples. These groups include CEOs from various organizations and industries (typically twelve to fifteen in a group) that come together to help each other solve problems, identify opportunities, and add a high dose of accountability. While there are some opportunities for non-CEOs to join groups like this (Vistage International has

groups for key executives and emerging leaders), you can also create internal mastermind groups where high-performing team members from across the company get together in the same way.

14. **Give them a project.** Identify a significant issue or opportunity for the organization and ask your high-performing team member to own a project focused on solving the problem or realizing the opportunity. This can be done as an individual or, like the accelerator session or Mars Team, as a group. For example, one of my clients in the software business gathered a group of high-performing team members and asked them to figure out how to cut their time to implementation by 50 percent.

15. **Help them plan their career.** Find out where they want to go in their career, inside or outside of your organization. How can you help them think it through? How can you help them come up with a plan to get there? How can you help them achieve their career goals?

16. **Re-recruit them.** Don't wait for an exit interview to find out why one of your high-performing team members is leaving. Do a stay interview. Let them know what a great job they're doing. Ask them what it would take to never leave. Get an understanding of what they love doing and figure out how they can do more of it. Understand what they hate doing and figure out how they can do less of it. Ask them what frustrates them and work with them to fix it. And here's a scary, but powerful, idea: ask them what it would take for them to leave. Maybe it's additional responsibility. Maybe it's more money. Whatever it is, better to know it now than after they're gone.

Again, this list is not exhaustive, but I hope it's a good start. My challenge to you is to have a ninety-day action plan focused on what you will do with and for each of your high-performing team members. Remember, the key point of the Talent Density System is to take massive action to improve strength of talent.

## WHAT TO DO NOW

Define actions for your high-performing team members:

1. Decide on a ninety-day objective. Objectives can include, but not be limited to, anything on the list above. It might be to re-recruit them, or teach them a new skill, or get them more exposure, etc. You can decide on this objective on your own or work collaboratively with the team member to make the best decision.
2. List the three to five most important actions necessary to accomplish that objective.
3. Determine a target date for each of those actions.
4. Take action!

### Actions for Medium-Performing Team Members

If you had a chance to do it all over again, would you enthusiastically rehire everyone on your team?

That's an easy question when it comes to team members performing at a high level... of course you would. It's also an easy question when it comes to team members performing at a low level (low producing or low culture fit)... of course you wouldn't.

What about your medium-performing team members? We probably wouldn't "enthusiastically" rehire them, but everyone can't be superstars, right? Isn't there always room for solid, mediocre performers?

#### Do We Need All High-Performing Team Members?

The short answer is "no." But the short answer is not clear enough.

While a goal of 100 percent high-performing team members might be unrealistic, I do believe we should strive to get there. Why not? Should we really be satisfied with someone performing at a medium level? I don't think so. We should always be striving to help someone improve their performance... for the benefit of the company, and the benefit of the team member. Remember, everyone can be high performing... somewhere. Let's help our team members become high performing, inside our company or out.

We're also *not* shooting for a bell-shaped curve: 20 percent high performing, 60 percent medium performing, and 20 percent low performing. That's a recipe for mediocrity at best and, more likely, failure and frustration. Remember, we're not comparing people to each other or force-ranking people in the Talent Assessment Model. We're assessing their performance against expectations. To have a great company, we need great people. That means a majority of our team members are meeting or beating our productivity and culture fit expectations.

In addition, there are two types of roles within our company where high performance is a requirement and mediocre performance is unacceptable. In these roles, team members should be performing at a high level, or at least have a strong potential to get there in the next three to six months.

Mediocre performance is unacceptable for any member of your leadership team. The massive impact each leader has cascading down through your organization and out to clients and vendors means high performance needs to be the standard. We can't become a great company if we allow mediocrity to permeate the organization from the highest level. I've never seen a high-performing team member work for a mediocre team member for very long without one of two things happening: they leave, or they stay and become mediocre themselves. It also impacts hiring. There's a saying that "A-players hire A-players, and B-players hire C-players." Now, I know the math doesn't work (someone must be hiring the B-players) and you already know I don't like the terms "A-player," "B-player," etc., but the logic is solid. Mediocre-performing team members tend to feel threatened when interviewing potential superstars. "Will they outshine me? Will they take my job?"

Mediocre performance is also unacceptable in the role for a "core" function. A core function is one that differentiates you in the marketplace. If you're a software company and your technology is a market differentiator for you, you can't afford to have mediocre engineers. If you're a marketing firm and you differentiate through your creative client solutions, you need high-performing team members in those positions. Now, in that same software company or marketing firm, your accounts payable department may not be a core function. You need to pay your bills but it's not a function that differentiates you in the marketplace. So, is it okay to have medium-performing team members in your accounts payable department? Likely yes. If you're the CFO or the manager of accounts payable, should you be striving to have your entire team perform at the highest levels? Of course you should. But if you've got team members performing at a medium level, should you fire them tomorrow because they're not performing at an elite level? Probably not.

With that understanding, let's discuss specific actions to take with and for your medium-performing team members. Remember, they're performing at a medium level because they're not producing at a high enough level and/or they're having occasional issues living your core values (culture fit).

1  Help them improve their productivity. What productivity expectations are they falling short on? How can you help them improve? Do you need to spend more time coaching them? Is there some training that might help? What about a mentor?

2  Help them improve their behavior to become a better culture fit. What core values are they occasionally having challenges with? How can you help them better understand the impact it's having on their performance, the team, and the company? How can you help them change their behavior? How can you help become a better role model for that behavior?

3  Change their role. If they're an excellent culture fit, but having challenges producing at a high level, a role change could skyrocket them to high performing in the snap of a finger. For example, you might have a salesperson who has an amazing

ability to initiate new relationships and develop those relationships, but just can't seem to close the deal. Is there a different role that better leverages their strengths and makes their weakness become irrelevant? Maybe an account manager or a strategic partnership role that requires their relationship-building strengths but doesn't require closing deals. To be clear, don't create a new role here just so you can best leverage someone's strengths. Changing roles is not always an option, but it's always something to think about. Change roles or create a new one only if it will add significant value to the organization.

4. Coach them out. If they're a member of the leadership team or part of a core function, do they have the potential to become high performing in the next three to six months? If you don't believe they do, it's time to have the difficult discussion—coach them out of the organization and allow them to become high performing in a different organization.

## WHAT TO DO NOW

Define actions for your medium-performing team members:

1. Decide on a ninety-day objective. Objectives can include, but are not limited to, anything on the list above. What will you do to help them improve productivity and/or their culture fit? Is changing their role an option? Is it time to coach them out of the organization and allow them to become high performing in a different organization?
2. List the three to five most important actions necessary to accomplish that objective.
3. Determine a target date for each of those actions.
4. Take action!

## Actions for Low-Performing Team Members

Actions for your low-performing team members are not complicated... but that doesn't mean they're not difficult. In fact, these situations, and the resulting actions, could be some of the hardest things we'll ever encounter as leaders. It's easy to say, "Let's fire the low performers!" but these are human beings. We hired them. We have some responsibility to nurture their growth. We have a responsibility to coach them. Having difficult conversations, and grappling with the potential for putting someone out of work, should not be taken lightly.

That being said, we need to set and defend a standard of excellence in our organizations. Therefore, we can't allow low-performing team members to continue to hurt the team and the company. We also can't allow them to continue to hurt themselves. Remember, everyone can perform at a high level... somewhere. By not acting, we're not giving them that chance.

### Actions for Low-Producing Team Members

Remembering that a team member is in this category because they're producing at a very low level, we have three options:

1. Help them improve their productivity. What productivity expectations are they falling short on? How can you help them improve? Do you need to spend more time coaching them? Is there some training that might help?

2. Change their role. As we discussed for medium performers, if they're an excellent culture fit, but having challenges producing at a high level, a role change to better leverage their strengths could skyrocket them to high performing in the snap of a finger.

3. Coach them out. If you've attempted to help them improve their productivity for ninety days, and it hasn't worked, and changing their role is not an option, coaching them out and allowing them to find an organization (and role) where they can flourish is the

right decision for you, the team, and the team member. I know ninety days sounds tough, but we can't afford to have a low-producing team member hurting the team for six, nine, or twelve months. We've all seen that happen and have seen the impact it has on the team. It should be unacceptable.

**Actions for Low Culture Fit Team Members**

A team member is in this category if they're frequently having problems living one or more of your company's core values. We have two options:

1. Help them improve their behavior to become a better culture fit. What core values are they frequently having challenges with? How can you help them better understand the impact it's having on the team? How can you help them change their behavior?

2. Coach them out. Someone who is not living your organization's nonnegotiable core values is worse than a bad fit, they're often toxic to your organization. No matter the level of their own productivity, they're hurting the performance and morale of those around them. If you've attempted to help them improve their culture fit for ninety days, and it hasn't worked, coaching them out and allowing them to find an organization that's a better fit is the right decision for you, the team, and the team member. Again, I realize ninety days sounds tight, but we can't afford to have someone with a low culture fit hurting the team for six, nine, or twelve months.

Notice there's no option for changing a low culture fit team member's role, as there was for a low-producing team member. This is because, while I've seen a role change dramatically impact productivity, I've almost never seen it impact culture fit.

There's another major difference between the low-producing and low culture fit categories...

Team members that are living the core values but are low producing tend to be coachable. Coachable to meet or beat your productivity expectations? Not necessarily... they may not have the capability. But they are typically willing to listen and strive to produce at a higher level.

On the other hand, team members with a low culture fit are typically *not* coachable. Trying to coach someone to live core values they're not already living is like trying to coach someone to become someone they're not. It's possible that maybe they're going through a tough life challenge right now or maybe they just need some maturing. Possible, but not probable. This is why it's so important to hire people who already live your core values. If they don't, it doesn't mean they're a bad person; it just means they're a bad fit for your organization. To be clear, if you put them on a ninety-day performance improvement plan (PIP) and threaten their job security, they'll change... until the threat is over, and then they'll revert to who they really are. Which, again, is not a bad person, just a bad fit.

One of the biggest leadership challenges is making the tough decision on a high-producing team member who's a poor culture fit.

I was facilitating a quarterly talent assessment meeting (more on that in Step 4) with one of my clients and we had a heated debate with the CEO about a salesperson who was consistently disrespectful and uncooperative with the customer service and operations teams.

"If you think I'm firing my best salesperson because he's not living the core values, you're crazy!" the CEO said.

I certainly understand the hesitancy to act on a high-producing team member. However, we need to consider the impact they're having on the people around them. We also need to understand the impact they're having on the credibility of your core values. If you let high-producing team members get away with not living your nonnegotiable core values, the values simply become an excuse to fire low producers. If you're going to let the core values be violated by some people but not by others, they take on a negative connotation at best, and become a joke at worst.

In this case, I coached the CEO to make one of two choices: have the difficult discussion and, potentially, coach the low culture fit salesperson out of the organization, or take the core values posters off the wall. Better not to communicate core values then to communicate them and not live them.

The decision to fire a team member is never taken lightly. However, I tend to see the opposite problem much more often: leaders hesitate and stall to have difficult discussions with lower performers and make resolving the issue more drawn out. This results in low performers sticking around organizations way too long, sometimes being shuffled from role to role.

When it comes to making the hard decisions about a low performer, here are some of the reasons or "excuses" leaders use to defend inaction:

**Excuse 1: We Owe This Person Our Loyalty**
"She was with me when I started. I've got to show some loyalty, don't I?"

Are you more loyal to this one person than you are to the rest of the organization they're dragging down? And, if you truly owe them loyalty, shouldn't you help them find another organization where they're a better fit?

**Excuse 2: We'll Be Short-Staffed**
This is the "low performer trap." There's no sense of urgency to find somebody else if the position is still filled, so you procrastinate. And here's my experience: When you transition that low performer out of the organization, the productivity around them, including your own, will go up. Meaning, you're not as short-staffed as you think you are.

**Excuse 3: We Can Do More Coaching**
"I'm not God," you might say. "I'm not all-knowing. How do I know if they're coachable?"

Be honest: You know if they're coachable. Is it possible there is one more coaching strategy that you haven't tried yet? Maybe. But are you willing to hold your organization hostage while you figure that out?

### Excuse 4: High Performers Cost Too Much

Sometimes when I'm doing this exercise with a leadership team, someone will raise a hand and say, "Do we really want all high performers? If everyone's a superstar, everyone's going to want more money and a promotion! We can't promote everyone." If you've got 90 percent superstars in your organization, trust me, you will be able to afford all the promotions, and all the increases in salaries, because you'll be growing so fast and so profitably.

### Excuse 5: We Might Get Sued

Are you letting the fear of lawsuits hold you back from building a great team?

Often, when we need to act, have a difficult conversation, or let go of a low performer, we hesitate—or worse, we're paralyzed by the threat of a lawsuit. Our lawyers have trained us to fear that any employee might sue us at any time.

Let me be clear, lawyers are just doing their jobs, and doing it well. Their job is to *protect* us from lawsuits, not to *grow* our business.

Sometimes, it makes sense to risk a lawsuit to grow your company.

If you're keeping a team member who's dragging down performance or is toxic to your organization, you might be protecting yourself from a lawsuit, but you're stifling your business's ability to grow.

Yes, we need to document discussions and specifics of low performance to reduce legal risk, but we can't let low performers hold us hostage.

Let's be brutally honest here: Most of these reasons (excuses) are code for "I'm really uncomfortable having difficult conversations, so I'd rather keep delaying things." Not only does this cause you indecision about coaching them out of the organization, but it also causes you to procrastinate about doing real coaching with these individuals. Everyone loses.

I have never heard a leader say, "I think I let go of that problem person too quickly." But I've heard "Why didn't I do that six months ago?" countless times.

And, sometimes the most powerful way to take care of your best people is to fire your worst.

What are you waiting for?

---

**WHAT TO DO NOW**

Define actions for your low-performing team members:

1. Decide on a ninety-day objective. Objectives can include, but not be limited to, anything on the list above.
2. List the three to five most important actions necessary to accomplish that objective.
3. Determine a target date for each of those actions.
4. Take action!

---

## Actions for High-Potential Team Members

I mentioned earlier that I see leaders use "potential" as an excuse way too often for people that aren't performing. Therefore, "potential" is not a component in determining whether someone is high performing, medium performing, low producing, or low culture fit.

However, there is a place for "potential" in the Talent Density System. It's helpful to identify those team members who have a high potential for growth into larger or more strategic roles within the company, so we can feed that potential.

First, we need to identify our high potentials. These typically, but not necessarily, come from our group of high-performing team members. We may have high-performing team members that have little desire or ability to do more. We also may have some medium-performing or even low-producing team members that have an enormous upside.

Here are the top five ways to spot individuals with the potential for larger or more strategic roles:

1. To observe their ability to think strategically, look for these signs:
   - They see the big picture and understand how their work fits into the broader organizational goals.
   - They anticipate future challenges and opportunities, offering proactive solutions.
   - They demonstrate curiosity about the company's vision, strategy, and industry trends.

   **Why it matters:** Strategic thinking is a key indicator of readiness for higher-level roles requiring complex decision-making and long-term planning.

2. To assess their learning agility, look for these signs:
   - They learn quickly from experiences, feedback, and mistakes.
   - They adapt to new challenges, technologies, or roles with ease.
   - They show a strong willingness to seek out new knowledge and improve skills continuously.

   **Why it matters:** High-potential individuals thrive in changing environments and demonstrate the capacity to grow beyond their current role.

3. To evaluate their leadership potential, look for these signs:
   - They naturally influence and inspire peers, even without formal authority.
   - They are collaborative, foster team cohesion, and handle conflicts constructively.
   - They demonstrate emotional intelligence by understanding and managing their emotions and those of others effectively.

   **Why it matters:** Leadership potential is crucial for roles requiring people management, team building, and organizational influence.

4  To monitor their performance consistency, look for these signs:
   - They consistently exceed expectations and deliver exceptional results.
   - They take ownership of their work and are dependable under pressure.
   - They maintain high-quality performance over time, and in diverse situations.

   **Why it matters:** Consistent high performers are more likely to succeed when entrusted with bigger responsibilities.

5  To gauge their drive and ambition, look for these signs:
   - They proactively seek out opportunities for growth, additional responsibilities, or leadership roles.
   - They express clear career aspirations aligned with the organization's future needs.
   - They show resilience, perseverance, and a strong sense of accountability.

   **Why it matters:** Motivation and ambition are critical for sustaining energy and focus in more demanding and strategic roles.

If you spot one or more of these clues to high potential, here are ten actions to help you nurture these team members, to maximize their contribution to the company and ensure their professional growth.

1  Create a customized development plan.

   **Action:** Collaborate with the individual to create a tailored development plan that aligns with their strengths, career aspirations, and organizational needs.

   **Why:** Personalization demonstrates investment in their growth and provides a clear road map for achieving goals.

2  Assign stretch assignments.

   **Action:** Give them challenging projects that push their limits, require cross-functional collaboration, and have visibility within the organization.

**Why:** Stretch assignments build skills, confidence, and visibility, accelerating their readiness for higher responsibilities.

3. Provide mentorship opportunities.

    **Action:** Pair them with a senior leader or external mentor who can provide guidance, share experiences, and broaden their perspective.

    **Why:** Mentorship fosters growth, expands networks, and enhances decision-making abilities.

4. Offer leadership training.

    **Action:** Enroll them in leadership development programs or workshops focused on skills like communication, strategic thinking, and emotional intelligence.

    **Why:** Early exposure to leadership tools prepares them to step into future leadership roles confidently.

5. Facilitate cross-functional exposure.

    **Action:** Rotate them through different departments or roles to give them a holistic understanding of the business.

    **Why:** Broad exposure strengthens their ability to see the bigger picture, improving strategic thinking and problem-solving.

6. Provide regular, constructive feedback.

    **Action:** Schedule regular check-ins to discuss their progress, areas for improvement, and career aspirations.

    **Why:** Feedback is essential for growth and keeps high-potential individuals engaged and aligned with company goals.

7. Involve them in strategic initiatives.

    **Action:** Include them in high-impact meetings, planning sessions, or special task forces.

    **Why:** Involvement in strategy helps them understand decision-making processes and prepares them for future leadership roles.

8. Recognize and reward achievements.

   **Action:** Publicly acknowledge their contributions, provide meaningful rewards, or offer new opportunities as recognition.

   **Why:** Recognition reinforces their value to the team and motivates continued excellence.

9. Encourage networking.

   **Action:** Provide opportunities for them to attend industry conferences, networking events, or internal leadership forums.

   **Why:** Building relationships with peers and leaders broadens their influence and fosters collaboration.

10. Create clear career pathways.

    **Action:** Discuss long-term career goals and outline potential paths within the company, including specific roles they can aim for.

    **Why:** Clear pathways ensure they feel valued and see a future within the organization, reducing the risk of turnover.

## Leveling Up Your Team

Now that I've laid out my recommended actions for each level of performance and your high potentials, let's discuss additional tactics to improve your team members' performance, regardless of the performance category they're in.

I recently worked with a client whose company was beating all of their growth goals. While that was great news, the CEO realized they needed to significantly level up their team's skills to keep the momentum going. Now, when most leaders think about boosting skills, the first thing that comes to mind is usually training. Yes, training is important. I've had some training sessions that genuinely changed the way I think or act. But we often give training too much credit.

Everyone has a different learning style, so traditional training isn't always effective for learning and applying the lessons. The training doesn't necessarily mirror the messy realities we face in our roles every day either. The best learning happens on the job, tackling real problems as they come.

Another thing about traditional training: It feels a bit detached from our daily grind. You're yanked out of your workday, plunked into a session, and then it's back to business as usual. This can make the training feel less relevant and harder to apply. Plus, there's hardly any follow-up. You check the box, maybe get a pat on the back, and that's it. How do we even know if it's making a dent in our performance, or the bottom line?

When we talk about upping our game in business, it's not just about piling on skills. It's about actually performing better across the board. And while I might sound a bit tough on training, I do think it has its place—it's just one piece of a much bigger puzzle. From my point of view, it's a small fraction of what you need to truly elevate your team's performance. We need to think bigger, integrating real-world learning and making sure these skills are genuinely taking root and driving results.

Here are twelve other ways to level up your team's skills and performance:

1 **Coach.** Coaching should be an integral part of daily work, not separate from it. It involves giving people the help they need by asking the right questions and guiding them through daily challenges and opportunities. Coach more and become a better coach. The best book I've ever read on coaching is *The Coaching Habit*, by Michael Bungay Stanier. If you haven't read it, do it! But finish this one first, of course.

2 **Improve the hiring process.** Elevating your team's performance starts with hiring the right people. Each new hire should raise the average skill level and performance, contributing positively to productivity and culture. I've previously recommended the hiring methodology of Topgrading, from the book *Who: The A Method for Hiring* by Geoff Smart and Randy Street. I highly endorse this book to anyone who would like to master this concept.

3. **Have the difficult discussion.** Learn to have tough conversations that are necessary for development. This involves being direct about expectations, performance issues, and the consequences of not meeting standards. More on this in the next section.

4. **Implement new tools.** Introduce tools or technologies that can automate tasks or enhance productivity, such as AI for decision-making or drafting content.

5. **Improve processes.** Streamline existing processes to remove inefficiencies. Assign clear ownership and accountability for critical processes like onboarding new clients or launching products.

6. **Strengthen your leadership.** Enhance your leadership skills to better motivate and inspire your team. What leadership books are you reading? Do you have a coach? Are you modeling and actively promoting the company's vision and values?

7. **Increase financial transparency.** The more top-line (revenue) and bottom-line (profitability) information you share, the more you empower your team to make healthy, profitable decisions. Be cautioned, however, that this additional information comes with a requirement to help your team become more financially literate so they can best utilize that information.

8. **Clarify the vision.** The clearer your vision, the better your team will be able to make effective decisions to realize that vision. This should include the "almost never changing" part of your vision—core purpose, BHAG (big hairy audacious goal), your three-year strategy and plan, and your annual priorities. Help your team understand what you want your organization to look like, sound like, and feel like in the future.

9. **Rationalize priorities.** Is your team spread too thin? Are you working on too many priorities at the same time? If I ask you what's most important and you list eight or twelve things, you don't know what's most important. Ensure you and your team

**Sometimes the most powerful way to take care of your best people** is to fire your worst.

---

are aligned around no more than three to five priorities for the year or quarter.

10. **Read a book together.** Pick a book that hones a skill relevant to your team and set a target completion date for the team. Set time aside to discuss the book in an actionable way. Instead of just having everyone summarize their learning, have them identify specific ideas they'd like to inject into the DNA of your team or company. Then, assign specific accountability for executing on ideas chosen to move forward.

11. **Facilitate group problem-solving.** Encourage team-based problem-solving to leverage diverse perspectives. This could be within specific functions like marketing or across functions involving multiple departments.

12. **Increase accountability.** Foster a culture where team members are held accountable for their actions and results. Ensure everyone understands the responsibilities, behaviors, and specific metrics expected of them. Also ensure you have a powerful communication rhythm, both in team meetings and one-on-ones, to hold team members accountable.

By weaving these twelve strategies into your management approach, you go beyond the conventional reliance on training sessions to develop a team that is skilled, cohesive, and motivated. This holistic method fosters an environment where continuous improvement is part of the daily routine, and each team member feels invested in the collective success of the organization. It helps create a dynamic team capable of adapting and thriving, even as business challenges and opportunities evolve.

### BURNING QUESTIONS

**How much should I be spending on training and talent development?**
Well, with this new approach to learning, does it matter? The time (and quality of that time) a leader spends on coaching, mentoring, feedback, and accountability is key, but is never included in this number. You can spend hundreds of thousands of dollars on training that may or may not be valuable. So, dollars spent is a poor indicator of doing the right things to grow your people.

## Let's Dump the Annual Performance Review

I told you this was coming. For most organizations, the worst part of the performance management process is the annual performance review. Companies like Apple and Microsoft retired them ages ago, but many companies are still holding on to this outdated and sometimes harmful process.

The biggest problem? Waiting twelve months to give feedback. Why on earth would you wait that long to tell someone how they're doing? You might think you're doing better by holding these reviews quarterly, but for many of you, that just means you're executing a flawed process four times per year. Imagine if Simone Biles's coach gave her feedback every few months, or if a baseball team reviewed their players' performance once per season. I can't imagine that on a little-league baseball team, let alone a professional one. Our companies need to be better than that.

Then there's the rating game. Not only is the feedback ridiculously late, but then we sometimes arbitrarily rate from one to five to fit a predefined organizational scoring curve. If you're handing out a "4" when your team member was expecting a "5," guess what? They're not listening to your feedback anymore; they're too busy fuming over the score. Why do we even need to put a number on it? Why not just say, "You're doing great, and here's a few areas you could work on"?

For the many organizations that still link the annual performance review with the salary/raise discussion, feel free to rank team members behind the scenes all you want. Put them on a bell-shaped curve, or do whatever works for your company. But don't share these rankings with team members—it will lead to defensiveness and it isn't necessary for their professional development.

So that's the problem with performance reviews: Instead of allowing our team members to focus on understanding and taking action on our feedback, we cause them to feel defensive, worrying about how every piece of criticism might hit their wallet and their pride in their work and their perceived value in the company.

Continue to conduct salary discussions annually or at whatever rhythms are in place, but it's vital to decouple these discussions from the review and talent development processes. The primary goal of a performance review should be to elevate team members from one performance level to a higher one—moving someone up and to the right on our Talent Assessment Model.

So, let's stop telling people what their "rating" is. Let's stop linking the annual performance review with salary. Or better yet, let's retire the annual performance review; it's just getting in the way of what we're really trying to do... grow our people, so we can grow our profit.

## The One-On-One Meeting Framework

Instead of annual, semiannual, or quarterly performance reviews, a more dynamic approach involves weekly one-on-one meetings with each of your direct reports. Each of these meetings should last thirty to forty-five minutes.

My suggested one-on-one framework incorporates two different types of meetings. Alternate between these meeting types each time you meet, as each one focuses on a different aspect of performance and development.

**Accountability and Feedback Meeting (Odd Weeks)**
As the name implies, the objective of these meetings is to hold your direct report accountable and give them important feedback on their performance.

This meeting should include a discussion of how they're performing against their productivity and culture fit expectations (via the expectations discussed back in Step 1), as well as performance on any ongoing projects or priorities they're accountable for. The one-on-one accountability discussion also allows for a deeper dive into issues and, when necessary, provides space for difficult discussions.

These sessions are also opportunities to provide feedback on both achievements and areas for improvement. It's a time to give recommendations, tips, and techniques to help make progress on areas of need and to better leverage their strengths. It may also be a time to do some goal setting or goal revisions. These sessions should give team members an understanding of how they're doing and what actions they need to take to get to the "next level." This meeting isn't meant to replace immediate feedback, which, of course, should be given as situations arise.

The agenda for this meeting is owned by the leader. For an accountability and feedback meeting template, go to my website strengthoftalent.com, and look in the Resources section.

The one-on-one meeting is not the only time to hold your direct reports accountable. Team members should be held accountable in a weekly team meeting as well. I call this meeting the "weekly accountability meeting" and its objective is to discuss progress on key priorities and commitments, resolve important issues, and hold team members accountable to their commitments. The detailed objectives and agenda for this meeting, as well as other critical parts of a successful planning and communication rhythm, are covered in my previous book, *Breakthrough Leadership Team*. Both one-on-one

**Trying to coach someone who doesn't live your core values** is like trying to coach someone to become someone they're not.

---

and team-level accountability discussions are critical. The team-level discussions are important so that the team can align on actions and hold one another accountable—the leader shouldn't be the only person to hold everyone on the team accountable.

### Coaching Meeting (Even Weeks)

These meetings are driven by a team member's needs, not the leader's. Coaching is a time for a direct report to say, "Here's where I need help," "Here's an issue I'm grappling with," "Help me move faster on this opportunity." The team member brings a topic or topics to the session, and the leader helps them explore solutions and strategies through guided questioning rather than direct advice. Asking questions, rather than giving advice, helps team members develop their own problem-solving skills, own the solution, and ensure you're solving the right problem. Leaders too often jump in to give advice without understanding what the real challenge is. As I've mentioned, the best book I've ever read on coaching is *The Coaching Habit*, by Michael Bungay Stanier.

The agenda for this meeting is owned by the direct report. It's important they prepare for the session beforehand, so they have a topic they'd like to discuss at the ready. The meeting should begin with you saying, "Okay, we've got thirty minutes for our coaching meeting, how do you want to use our time?" If your direct report says, "I don't know, what do you want to talk about?," you won't have a very effective session. I learned a specific set of preparation questions from my amazing coach David Herdlinger of Kashbox Coaching. It's called the Coaching Period-in-Review and consists of the following questions (my clients send the answers to the questions to me before each one of my coaching sessions with them):

1. What has happened since we last spoke?
2. What am I proud of having accomplished since we last spoke?
3. Where am I stuck?
4. What opportunities are available to me right now?
5. Where do I need the greatest support from you right now?
6. What would be the best way to coach me today?

The first two questions make it easier for you to jump right into coaching. You don't have to start by saying, "How's every-thing going?" The last four questions help your direct report think through what they want to focus on during the coaching session.

If your direct report comes to several coaching sessions unsure or unable to come up with something to focus the coaching on, it's a sign that there may be something deeper going on:

1 They're fearful of being honest about where they need help. This means you need to find ways to create a more trusting environment, so they feel comfortable being vulnerable. One way to do this is to be more vulnerable with them. If you trust them enough to share where you need help, they might begin to trust you more as well.

2 You're not challenging them enough, so they don't need help. Therefore, challenge them by raising the bar on expectations or challenge them to learn something new.

3 They don't know what they don't know. In other words, they need help, but they're not seeing things clearly enough to see it. Help them see it.

4 They're not coachable. They may be reluctant to ask for help because they're stuck in their ways. Or maybe their ego won't let them admit when they need help. This can be a dangerous issue. People who aren't coachable are unlikely to grow and scale as your team and company grow and scale.

To find a template that your direct reports can use to prepare for a coaching meeting, go to my website strengthoftalent.com, and look in the Resources section.

This new approach could revolutionize how we handle performance feedback, making it a powerful tool for growth rather than a dreaded, ineffective ritual. Let's make the shift, ditch those outdated, ineffective reviews, and start actually helping our teams improve continuously. Why not start a trend? By next year, maybe we'll have seen the last of those dreaded annual reviews.

## Having Difficult Conversations

As leaders, we absolutely must master the art of having difficult conversations. If we don't get this right, one of two scenarios typically unfolds.

The first scenario is that we jump into a conversation unprepared, especially when we need to give tough feedback—maybe someone has let us down or they're not pulling their weight. If we're not skilled in handling these discussions, we might just blurt out our feelings or accusations, often making the situation worse.

The second, less obvious scenario is avoidance. We avoid these necessary confrontations out of fear. We put off the conversation, hoping the problem will go away, but it only festers. With time, it continues to grow until we can't ignore it anymore. When we finally bring it up, it's a massive issue that blindsides the other person, who wonders, "Why didn't you mention this earlier?"

To be effective, impactful leaders, we must become adept at these tough conversations. This involves not only knowing how to conduct a one-on-one discussion but also managing group discussions and ensuring they're productive rather than destructive.

Before diving into those skills, it's important to adopt what I call an "umbrella mindset," centered on the "law of positive intent." The law of positive intent simply says everyone is doing the best they can with the resources they have. That does *not* mean everybody's doing the right thing. They may not have the resources you have. They may not have the knowledge you have, or maybe they know something you don't know. But very often what we do when we are in a debate or in conflict with someone else is we assume negative intent. We assume this person did something wrong on purpose. Now, I don't know about you, but I've never known anyone who woke up in the morning and said, "What can I screw up today?" Maybe you have, but let me ask you this: How often has assuming negative intent actually helped you solve a problem? Assuming negative intent makes you frustrated and closes you off from creative answers. Assuming positive intent makes you curious. It opens your mind to at least try to find an answer. So, whether you truly believe the other person has positive intent or not, it's still a more empowering focus than assuming they're evil people.

Here's how you can handle these tough conversations more effectively, with a process adapted from Kevin Lawrence's insights in *Your Oxygen Mask First*. (The first step is mine, but steps two through five are his.)

The steps are straightforward and practical:

1 Set clear goals. Before you even start, be clear about what you hope to achieve. This isn't about making the other person feel bad; it's about resolving issues constructively. Your goal might be to solve a problem, or it might simply be to take the first step in improving your relationship.

2 Invite them to the conversation. Let them know you need to discuss something important: "Hey John, there's something important I need to speak with you about...." It's an easy way to start and sets them up for a serious conversation.

3 Start with the facts—without inserting your feelings or judgments. "You always disrespect me in meetings" is not a statement of fact. It's an opinion. Instead, describe the actual thing that happened: "In this morning's meeting, you interrupted me three times." This will help steer the person away from defensiveness and make the discussion less combative.

4 Share feelings and impact. After presenting the facts, explain how the situation makes you feel. "When you interrupt me, it makes me feel like you don't respect my opinion." This helps the other person understand your perspective without feeling attacked. They may say, "I didn't mean to make you feel that way." But it's tough for them to argue that you don't feel that way. Here, you might also share the impact their behavior is having on you, the team, or their own career progression. Allow them to share their feelings and impact as well.

5 Agree on a resolution. Now that both parties understand the facts, feelings, and impact, you have the foundation to work

together to find a solution. While you might come to the discussion with a proposed resolution, it's important to hear the other person out as well. "I'm sorry I interrupted you, but sometimes it takes you so long to get your ideas out, and it's frustrating because I just want to get to the point!" That's important for you to know, because the resolution may be, "Hey, I will agree to get to the point more quickly if you'll agree to give me a little bit more space."

While this process is not guaranteed to solve every problem, it will help dramatically improve the chances of making progress toward a positive outcome.

Now, who do you need to have a difficult conversation with?

### WHAT TO DO NOW

While you're motivated, schedule one-on-ones with each of your direct reports now.

1. Determine whether your meetings will be weekly or every two weeks. Weekly is recommended, but every two weeks is an appropriate start if one-on-ones are a new habit for you or your organization.
2. Communicate the importance of these meetings to your team. Explain the difference between the two types of meetings (accountability and feedback, and coaching) and stress the importance of their preparation for each. Share the prework forms for each meeting as well.
3. Create these as repeating meetings (same day and time) every week (or biweekly) and send these as calendar invitations to each of your team members. Remember to alternate between the two different types of meetings. Put the meeting type in the title and attach the appropriate template so you both can prepare.

## BURNING QUESTIONS

**Are you kidding? I'm too busy as it is, how can I make time for these one-on-one meetings?**
If you're struggling to fit these meetings into your schedule—if it feels like there are just too many people to meet with—it might be a sign you've got too many direct reports. Or maybe, it's just about making these one-on-ones a higher priority. Remember, the #1 driver of profit growth is people growth. Nothing should take precedence over developing your team. Make the time. The return on investment will ensure you get the time back, and then some, by ensuring your team members are more effective. I promise!

If you truly don't have time for productive one-on-one meetings with each of your direct reports every week, then at worst, have these meetings every other week. If that's still a problem, here's a bit of tough love...

If you aren't willing to make the time to have quality, weekly (or at worst, biweekly) one-on-one meetings with your direct reports, you shouldn't have direct reports. If you're saying you literally don't have the time, you probably mean you are not willing to prioritize these one-on-one meetings over other tasks. As a leader, strengthening your team's talent is your number one priority. I can't imagine anything more important than that. The one-on-one meetings are a major part of the recipe for turning low performers into high performers—for moving people up and to the right of the Talent Assessment Model.

## Quick Review

We're doing the wrong things in how we take action with and for our team members:

- We don't prioritize "taking action" on team member performance
- We don't know how to effectively impact performance
- We put too much onus on whether we hired right or not
- We overinvest in low-performing team members
- We don't have the difficult conversations or make the difficult decisions
- We make decisions based on the perceived immaturity of our people

There are six key philosophies for acting:

- The #1 driver of profit growth is people growth
- If you want a great company, you need a great team
- Everyone can be high performing... somewhere
- Fire fast, hire slow
- Overinvest in high-performing team members
- Maybe you didn't hire wrong; you're just not leading right

You have several possible actions for high-performing team members:

- Challenge them
- Raise the bar
- Increase their responsibility
- Invest in them
- Promote them
- Ask them to mentor or coach someone else
- Reward them
- Recognize them
- Remove barriers
- Give them more exposure
- Conduct an accelerator session
- Create a Mars Team

- Help them join a mastermind
- Give them a project
- Help them plan their career
- Re-recruit them

You have four possible actions for medium-performing members:

- Help them improve their productivity
- Help them improve their behavior to become a better culture fit
- Change their role
- Coach them out (if they're in a differentiating role or a member of your senior leadership team)

You have three possible actions for low-producing team members:

- Help them improve their productivity
- Change their role
- Coach them out

You have two possible actions for low culture fit team members:

- Help them improve their behavior to become a better culture fit
- Coach them out

You have five ways to spot high-potential team members:

- Observe their ability to think strategically
- Assess their learning agility
- Evaluate their leadership potential
- Monitor their performance consistency
- Gauge their drive and ambition

You have ten possible actions for high-potential team members:

- Create a customized development plan
- Assign stretch assignments
- Provide mentorship opportunities

- Offer leadership training
- Facilitate cross-functional exposure
- Provide regular, constructive feedback
- Involve them in strategic initiatives
- Recognize and reward achievements
- Encourage networking
- Create clear career pathways

Here are twelve ways to level up your team:

- Coach
- Improve the hiring process
- Have the difficult discussion
- Implement new tools
- Improve processes
- Strengthen your leadership
- Increase financial transparency
- Clarify the vision
- Rationalize priorities
- Read a book together
- Facilitate group problem-solving
- Increase accountability

I also give you the framework for the two types of weekly one-on-one meetings:

- Accountability and feedback meeting
- Coaching meeting

Here is how to have difficult conversations:

- Set clear goals
- Invite them to the conversation
- Start with the facts
- Share feelings and impact
- Agree on a resolution

Go to my website strengthoftalent.com to access my book resources, where you'll find these helpful tools:

- A form to document the actions you're committing to take for each of your direct reports, along with a direct reports actions checklist
- Meeting prep worksheets for both the accountability and feedback meeting and coaching meeting

To help better document and track your actions to improve the strength of talent for each member of your team, go to talentdensitysystems.com to learn about this system and claim your free three-month access to the tool.

STEP 4

# DRIVE ACCOUNTABILITY

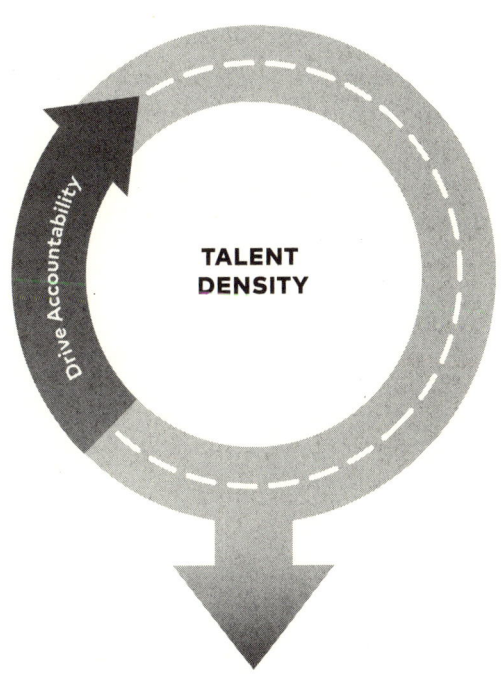

## Driving Accountability—the Wrong Way

When a team member is not performing, we tend to assume we hired wrong. That may be the case. In fact, there are dozens of great books focused on improving the hiring process. However, just as often, we hire right but develop wrong... or don't develop at all. This "we just hired wrong" mindset takes our focus off providing the right tools to develop strength of talent as well as holding our leaders accountable for growing the people they already have.

As a result, we drive accountability for the wrong things or, most often, don't drive any real accountability for growing our people.

Here are just some of the shortcomings I've seen from organizations related to driving accountability for building strength of talent:

### We Have No Clear Definition of Accountability

"People don't follow through on their commitments! How do I hold them accountable? Do I just have to fire everybody?"

I've heard this complaint from dozens of leaders. Where I typically start to dissect the problem is by checking on their definition of accountability. (Often, it's confusing and unclear.)

- "It's something you're responsible for"
- "It's a feeling of ownership"
- "It's measuring whether what you did worked"
- "It's the ramifications of your actions"

While none of these answers sound horribly wrong, all of these answers were provided by the same leader! If I ask the leadership table, each leader generally responds differently. Referring back to Step 1, unclear expectations lead to unacceptable results. So, let's be clear.

Part of the confusion is that we tend to use the words "accountable" and "responsible" interchangeably. Despite dictionary.com's similar definitions for these two words, it's vital to differentiate them.

Here are the distinctions my clients find helpful:

- **Accountable** means you own the function. It is your job to strategize, plan, and manage the performance of this function. *One and only one person is accountable.* Having more than one person accountable for a function means no one is accountable for that function.

- **Responsible** means it's your job to roll up your sleeves and get the work done. This could be one person, one thousand, or any number in between. The person accountable may also be responsible for the function, but not necessarily.

Key point: *One* person is accountable. Who should that one person be? We'll get to that in this chapter.

### We Approach Team Member Performance Assessment and Improvement as a Lone Effort

In most organizations, assessing performance and taking action to improve performance is a lone effort. But we can't do it ourselves. Increasing strength of talent is a team sport.

We can't effectively set expectations for our team members without the help of our peers. How can we set sales targets without understanding our production capacity? How can we set a target for the number of marketing qualified leads if we don't know our sales targets?

We can't effectively assess the performance of our team members without the help of our peers. We know how our team members treat us, but we don't see their behavior with other departments or individuals. Some organizations use 360-degree evaluations to ensure they're getting feedback from peers; however, those tend to be conducted once per year, at most. We need this feedback much more frequently.

We can't effectively define actions to improve the performance of our team members without the help of our peers. We don't have a monopoly on the best ways to coach and develop the members of our team. Our peers will have ideas and insights we may not see.

We can't effectively drive accountability without feeling accountable to the other members of our team.

## We Look at Human Resources Too Tactically

How does it feel to be called a human resource?

It doesn't infuse you with a good dose of pride and confidence, does it? It makes you feel like a cog in a machine. But your team is *not* an assembly line.

In fact, we need to stop calling it "human resources"!

Here's why I feel so strongly about this: The words "human resources" have *nothing* to do with creating a great experience for your team—nor with attracting, developing, and retaining talent.

And I get it. It comes from the administrative part of the job that makes sure payroll is taken care of, benefits are paid, everyone's name, address, birthday, etc. is in the system, and performance reviews are completed on time (*don't* get me started again on performance reviews!). Can a simple thing like the label of a department really get in the way of your talent development?

I have two clients making this change right now. They each have a perfectly capable head of human resources in place, but they realize that to truly scale and create a healthier business, they need someone with a different skill set. Someone with a more strategic approach to talent development.

Their first step? They're changing the function name from human resources to talent development.

In your company, you might call it chief people officer, SVP of employee experience, or VP of talent development.

**Measure people growth with the same rigor** as you measure profit growth.

---

Call it whatever you want. But make it about *people*.

Make it about talent development instead of benefits, payroll, and tracking people's information.

Often, what happens after you do that is you realize no one is truly focusing on talent development. So you get serious about it. You start asking questions:

- How can we improve our chances of hiring the best people?
- How can we better assess the talent on our team?
- What coaching and development do we need to put in place to help people get to the next level?

And yes, sometimes changing the label leads to changing the person too. Because if you just give your HR director a different name, you haven't solved the problem.

If you keep calling it "human resources," you'll continue to think about it the old way.

No, changing the title is not the solution. But it's a necessary first step to set you off on the right path—a step that can create a ripple effect of long-lasting and profound change in your company.

### We Don't Have a Measure for Strength of Talent

I've made the following statement several times in this book: The #1 driver of profit growth is people growth.

If that's true, we have a big problem. We've all heard the cliché "you can't manage what you don't measure." It's a cliché because it's true.

Now, of course we measure profitability. If I asked you what your net profit is, you'd be able to quickly give me an answer to the tenth of a percent: "We're 10.3 percent over plan and 15.4 percent over last year." But if I asked you how you're doing with people growth, you'd stumble a bit and say something like, "Pretty good." "Pretty good" doesn't cut it! We need a measure so that we can benchmark where we are, set goals to improve, and hold each other accountable for that improvement.

*We need to measure people growth with the same rigor as revenue or profit growth.*

How do we do that? I'll be showing you later in this chapter.

## The Right Way: Leadership Accountability

As a company, team, or individual leader, we can set expectations, assess performance, and act (the first three steps of this five-step framework) and still ultimately fail if we don't drive accountability. Without effective accountability, the urgent fire drills will eventually overtake the important work of strengthening our team's talent. Without accountability, we'll struggle to keep rolling when times get tough. Without accountability, we'll feel like we can never win the race—we just keep running without a finish line in sight.

We need to drive leadership accountability for more than its typical key performance indicators—number of sales meetings, closing ratio, etc. We need leaders to be accountable for strengthening the talent of their teams by working with each team member to improve their productivity and their behaviors that lead to a stronger culture fit. For most companies, that's an afterthought. We need to make it the highest priority.

But what, specifically, do we need to hold leaders accountable for?

### Assessing the Performance of the Team Accurately

While I've seen leaders be too harsh on their team and, as a result, assess individual performance at a much lower level than reality would dictate, I more often see leaders overestimating an individual's performance. They might do this by creating productivity expectations that are too low and/or overlooking behavioral issues impacting culture fit. This may be an honest mistake, or it may be a way to escape from the difficult discussions and decisions required to deal with low-performing team members.

For this process to work, our assessments need to be accurate. Not perfect, but accurate. Leaders need to be challenged to justify both unusually high and low assessments. In addition, we need to do a reality check on a leader's assessment. As an example, if we're consistently missing our client retention goals, and our VP of service assesses all team members as high performing, we likely have an inaccurate assessment. Changing expectations may also result from changes to your business strategy, competitive challenges, or economic factors.

### Taking Action with Each of the Direct Reports

Step 3 details many of the actions necessary to improve strength of talent. We need to hold our leaders accountable for those actions specific to each category of performance as well as the more general actions to level up their team. It's too easy to focus on the fire drill of the day. Too easy to focus on what's urgent and leave what's important to another day… another day that never comes. Taking action with your direct reports is almost never urgent, but almost always important.

Remember this is not just about taking action on low-performing team members. In fact, the most important actions are more often the actions you take with and for your high-performing team members. Lastly, don't forget to hold leaders accountable for conducting weekly one-on-one accountability and feedback as well as coaching sessions with each of their direct reports.

### Raising the Bar

You might lead a team where everyone is producing at a 9 or 10 out of 10. Congrats, that's great! It's time to raise the bar. If a company is not growing, it's dying. If we're hitting all our targets, let's shoot higher. You'll never know what you can achieve unless you try. And the targets you set when you were a twenty-million-dollar business may not cut it anymore, now that your goal is fifty million dollars. Recall that the first action I recommended for high-performing team members was to challenge them. As I've mentioned, I've seen more great people leave out of boredom than anything else. It's not enough to say, "Keep up the good work." Sometimes it's necessary to redefine what good work looks like. We need to hold our leaders accountable for raising the bar.

### Providing Feedback on Peers' Direct Reports

While we can measure the productivity of our team members, we can't always see the impact they have on others. An accounting manager may treat the CFO with great respect but be condescending to the sales team. A salesperson may be a great team player in front of the VP of sales but be uncooperative with the service team. These behaviors may not impact that team member's productivity, but their behaviors absolutely impact the productivity of others and the overall culture of the organization.

Therefore, leaders need to be held accountable for communicating what they and team member peers see, both good and bad. I created a specific step in the Talent Density System called the quarterly talent assessment meeting (QTAM) to ensure this happens at least quarterly, and we'll be looking at that next. However, this should happen much more often than that... as close to real time as possible.

### Increasing the Talent Density of the Team

Actions are important, but results are what we're after. So, in addition to holding leaders accountable for all actions previously mentioned, we need a way to hold them accountable for results. We need a tool to ensure the actions are having the impact we need them to have—improving strength of talent on our teams. After we look at the QTAM, I'll show you that tool: the Talent Density Indicator.

## The Quarterly Talent Assessment Meeting (QTAM)

The secret sauce of the Talent Density System is the quarterly talent assessment meeting.

As I mentioned earlier, one of the problems with current talent assessment processes is that they're done behind closed doors. I

**If you don't measure strength of talent,** you won't have strength of talent.

---

know some organizations drive group discussions about their team members, but often managers use this as a time to position and protect their team members so they can get the higher rankings and/or salary increases.

The QTAM is the truth serum and driver of accountability. It will ensure effective involvement from your peers, driving the discussion and debate required to ensure accurate assessments. There's nothing like a good challenge from one of your peers to inject more honesty into your assessments:

- "How can your whole sales team be high in productivity if we're not meeting our company sales goals?"
- "Tell me again why you've rated him high in culture fit when he refuses to take ownership of his mistakes?"

There's also nothing like a good challenge from your peers to drive more accountability for taking action:

- "Didn't you say last quarter you were going to change her role to better leverage her strengths? Her role never changed... what happened?"
- "That's the second high-performing team member that dropped to medium performing in the past three quarters. What's going on?"

These conversations are an incredibly powerful part of the entire process. The QTAM puts the goal of strengthening talent front and center each quarter. And, since the #1 driver of profit growth is people growth, that focus is critical to your success.

My clients facilitate the QTAM as part of their regularly scheduled quarterly planning meeting. The quarterly planning meeting is typically one to two days, and the QTAM portion takes about sixty to ninety minutes.

#### QTAM Attendees

If you're the CEO, attendees should be you and your direct reports—basically, your leadership team. In the meeting, these leaders will assess their direct reports. I don't recommend assessing people who are present in the meeting. Therefore, the CEO should not be assessing their direct reports (the leadership team) in that QTAM. Their assessment should happen separately with the help of a coach, mentor, or accountability partner from outside the organization.

This process should eventually cascade down to all levels of the organization (see Step 5), resulting in separate QTAMs for each level within a team. For example, the CFO would be in the senior leadership team QTAM as a participant and a finance team QTAM as the leader, attended by their direct reports. The controller (who directly reports to the CFO) would attend the finance team QTAM as a participant and an accounting team QTAM as the leader, attended by their direct reports (if they have direct reports who also have direct reports).

#### The QTAM Process (Done Every Quarter, Hence the "Q")

This process will require filling out the Talent Assessment Form (see the table that follows). To successfully carry out this assessment, follow these steps:

1. List the names of all team members you are assessing on the Talent Assessment Form. If you are the VP of operations and you have five direct reports, each would be listed. (Again: the CEO is not evaluating members of the leadership team in this meeting. Those assessments are made privately by the CEO in consultation with someone external to the team. It could be a business coach, mentor, or any type of accountability partner.)

2. Mark the productivity score and culture fit score for each of your direct reports based on the process in the "Completing the Assessment" section in Step 2.

3. Have each member of the leadership team write the initials for each person on a small sticky note, along with their scores (productivity first, culture fit second). If you were evaluating Mike Goldman, you would write "MG 8, 9."

4. Have each leader, one at a time, share their scores with the others so the leadership team knows the talent everyone else has on their departmental team. For instance, the head of operations might say, "I gave Joe Bennett, the director of warehousing, an 8 in productivity and an 8 in culture fit. Joe is performing at a medium level." Then the head of operations puts the note with "JB 8, 8" on the Talent Assessment Form. Then she does the same for the rest of her direct reports.

5. The other leaders support or challenge one another's scores as needed as each is presented. Leadership team members may have experiences with or information regarding others' teams that their fellow leaders haven't heard: "Wait a minute. How can you give Bob a 10 for culture fit? I saw him screaming at somebody out in the hallway yesterday." You can't discuss every person because you'll be there all day, but this is the right time to bring up conflicting assessments and questions. Continue this process until all team member assessments have been shared and challenged.

6. Discuss and brainstorm actions for your high-performing team members. To save time, you might review all the different actions a leader might take with and for them, and then leave it to each individual leader to identify actions for their specific direct reports (as opposed to discussing each person, in detail). Use the recommended actions from Step 3 ("Actions for High-Performing Team Members" section) as a starting point. While this discussion is taking place, leaders document the actions they're committing to take with and for their high-performing team members on the Talent Assessment Form. Leaders should have a different action plan for each individual. One may be

overdue for a promotion, while another may need recognition. Each quarter, these leaders should have an action plan to mentor, coach, challenge, or reward these high performers.

7 Discuss and brainstorm actions for your medium-performing team members. Again, to save time, you might review all the different actions a leader might take with and for them, and then leave it to each individual leader to identify actions for their specific direct reports. Use the recommended actions from Step 3 ("Actions for Medium-Performing Team Members" section) as a starting point. While this discussion is taking place, leaders document the actions they're committing to take with and for their medium-performing team members on the Talent Assessment Form. Leaders should have a different action plan for each individual. One may need to further develop their collaboration with the customer service team, while another might need coaching on how to close more sales, and a third might need a role change.

8 Discuss and brainstorm actions for each of your low-producing team members. No saving time here, as these team members should be discussed individually. Use the recommended actions from Step 3 ("Actions for Low-Producing Team Members" section) as a starting point. While this discussion is taking place, leaders document the actions they're committing to take with and for their low-producing team members on the Talent Assessment Form.

9 Discuss and brainstorm actions for each of your low culture fit team members. Again, no saving time here—these team members should be discussed individually, not as a group. Use the recommended actions from Step 3 ("Actions for Low Culture Fit Team Members" section) as a starting point. While this discussion is taking place, leaders document the actions they're committing to take with and for their low culture fit team members on the Talent Assessment Form.

10. Discuss and brainstorm actions for any high-potential team members identified. These can be discussed both individually, and as a group. While this discussion is taking place, leaders document the actions they're committing to take with and for their high-potential team members on the Talent Assessment Form.

11. The last step is to widen the perspective by looking at the team's strength of talent as a whole. How do you feel about the team's performance? Did you see an improvement from last quarter? What improvements would you like to see before the next QTAM?

| Talent Assessment Form | | | |
|---|---|---|---|
| Team Member | Productivity Score (1–10) | Culture Fit Score (1–10) | Action Plan |
|  |  |  |  |
|  |  |  |  |
|  |  |  |  |
|  |  |  |  |

**A Note About Low Performers**

Steps 8 and 9 in the QTAM process (actions for low performers) are the hardest steps. They're hard because we're challenging ourselves and our leaders to make decisions that, sometimes, impact people's lives. Making the decision to transition a low performer out of the organization is one of the hardest parts of being a leader. But it's also one of the most crucial for team and business growth.

As previously stated, leaders keeping low performers on the team too long out of a misplaced sense of loyalty hurts the team, the company, you, *and* the low performer.

To further a strong sense of accountability and challenge leaders to make the tough decisions, here are the specific words I use when facilitating through the discussion of an individual low performer in steps 8 and 9.

Me: "I see Joe is down in low-performance territory. Can we coach him up or do we need to coach him out?"

Leader: "I still think I should work with Joe on this."

Now, of course, it's okay to say the answer is coaching. These are human beings. You hired them. You have some responsibility to take care of them. But here's where I drive accountability home.

Me: "Great. Here's my challenge to you. You know this is a quarterly talent assessment, right? So that means ninety days from now, we'll be doing this again. So go coach them, but if in ninety days they're still a low performer, and you still believe they need more coaching, *you might be the C-player*"—I know, I broke my rule about labeling here, but I get a bit emotional about this. Sorry, I won't do it again.

It's likely going to feel difficult and uncomfortable, but can you afford a low performer hurting the team and business performance for six months, nine months, twelve months, two years? We've all witnessed this too many times.

Here's another scenario I see much too often.

Me: "I see Joe is down in low-performance territory. Can we coach him up or do we need to coach him out?"

Leader: "I still think I should work with Joe on this."

Me: "How long has this been going on?"

Leader: "Wow, it's been about a year now."

Me: "A year? And you still think he needs more coaching?"

Leader: "I've gotta coach him because I haven't really talked to him about it yet."

This happens all the time and it's unacceptable. It's leadership malpractice.

The QTAM will help ensure this never happens again.

## BURNING QUESTIONS

**How do I get my team to be more consistent in their evaluation of talent? How do I keep leaders from wanting to protect their low performers?**

The QTAM process is the primary way to make this happen. Encouraging your leaders to challenge each other on their assessments, as well as the resulting actions, will ensure that consistency and honesty increase over time. I've facilitated QTAM sessions where a company missed their sales targets for three quarters in a row, and yet, their VP of sales assessed 80 percent of her sales team as high performers. The QTAM provides the vehicle for other leaders to challenge the VP of sales and get her to rethink her assessment. I've also been a part of QTAM sessions where leaders debated the definition of a core value. Productive debates on these questions are another way to ensure consistency, accuracy, and honesty. A deeper dive on ways to accomplish this is in Step 5.

**Is the CEO's assessment of their direct reports discussed in the QTAM with the leadership team?**

No. This would mean the CEO would have to share their assessment of the leadership team in front of the entire leadership team. I believe that's awkward and inappropriate. To ensure the CEO is being challenged and held accountable, I suggest they execute a version of the QTAM with a coach or accountability partner from outside of the organization.

## The Talent Density Indicator

How do you know all of this is working? You measure it, of course. Here is your gold standard for understanding the strength of the talent in your organization: the Talent Density Indicator (TDI).

Having a powerful way to measure strength of talent each quarter dramatically increases our ability to drive accountability.

*If you don't measure strength of talent, you won't have strength of talent.*

Before we get into how the TDI is calculated, let's review why it's so important.

There are two different types of key performance indicators (KPIs), as I discussed in Step 1:

- **Lagging indicators** are measures of results. Revenue is a lagging indicator. EBITDA is a lagging indicator. Anything on your P&L or balance sheet is a lagging indicator.

- **Leading indicators** are measures of activities that drive results. For example, the number of meetings with decision-makers might be a strong leading indicator to drive revenue.

It's difficult to impact a lagging indicator directly. If I say, "We need to increase revenue by 20 percent," there's no magic revenue dial to turn. It's not clear what we should do to increase revenue. However, if we say, "Let's increase our number of meetings with key decision-makers," our actions become much clearer. That *is* a dial we can turn.

Why am I explaining all this? *Because the TDI is the master of all leading indicators!*

Remember the three characteristics of a great company: consistent top- and bottom-line growth, a growing, fulfilling environment for all team members, and having a significant impact on the world.

The Talent Density Indicator is the #1 driver of all those characteristics.

If you want to know why you're not growing top and bottom line, the first place to look is your TDI. You want to know why you don't have a growing, fulfilling environment, look at your TDI. You want to know why you're not having the impact you want to have. Look to your TDI.

So, let's talk about the calculation. It's simple, yet very powerful. It's your percent high-performing team members minus your percent low-performing team members:

**TDI = High Performing % – (Low Producing % + Low Culture Fit %)**

Let's take it step by step.

1. Count the number of people you assessed that are high performing.

2. Calculate the percent of people that are high performing by dividing that number into the total number of people you assessed. For example, if you assessed five people and one of them was high performing, you have 20 percent high-performing team members.

3. Count the number of people you assessed that are low performing (either low producing or low culture fit).

4. Calculate the percent of people that are low performing by dividing that total number into the total number of people you assessed. For example, if you assessed five people and one was low producing and another one was low culture fit (for a total of two), you have 40 percent low-performing team members.

5. Calculate your TDI by subtracting your low-performing percent (in this example, 40 percent) from your high-performing percent (in this example, 20 percent). That would involve subtracting 40 percent from 20 percent, which equals a TDI of negative 20 percent.

Notice your result will be anywhere from negative 100 percent to positive 100 percent.

**We want to play a game** when we have a chance to win.

---

If 100 percent of your direct reports are performing at a high level, 100 percent minus zero is positive 100 percent.

If 100 percent of your direct reports are performing at a low level, subtracting 100 percent from 0 percent is negative 100 percent.

So, we now have a measure. But what do we do with it?

### Use TDI as a Benchmark and to Set Quarterly Targets

Once we have this measure, we have a benchmark. We understand where we are now. Now we can set targets each quarter for what kind of TDI improvement you want to see. Benchmarks should be measured, and targets should be set at the company level, function level (sales, marketing, finance, etc.), and for each leader.

*We need to measure people growth with the same rigor as revenue or profit growth.*

Do you have a plan for making these improvements? Of course, you do... if you did the work in Step 3.

### Use TDI as a Gauge of the Truth

There will be times when your TDI is high but, as a company or a team, you're underperforming. For example, I was facilitating the QTAM with one of my clients that was consistently missing their client retention targets. Their COO rated the client service director as high performing. There was an obvious disconnect between the COO's view of his team's performance and the actual results they were getting. The rest of the leadership team (with the CEO taking the lead) called BS on that and challenged the COO—who, it turns out, was more focused on protecting his people than making an honest assessment. That's the last time he made that mistake.

### Establish Ownership

Who's accountable for the TDI? Who on the team owns performance against that measure?

There are two answers to that question:

At the company level, there should be one person accountable. While there's no one right answer, I've seen it naturally fall either to the CEO or the leader of your talent function (this could be the chief people officer, VP of talent development, VP of human resources, or similar title). If the leader of your talent function is strategic (responsible for more than the tactical HR functions like benefits, payroll, etc.), I believe they should be accountable. If you don't have a strategic talent function, the CEO is the best choice.

At the function or team level, each leader should be accountable for the TDI for their team. In other words, the VP of finance would be accountable for the accumulated TDI for the entire finance department. Every leader's number one priority should be growing strength of talent on their teams. Therefore, each function or team should have a TDI benchmark as well as a target for the next quarter.

Based on this, any team member that leads others must have the TDI as one of the productivity expectations we set back in Step 1.

**Learn from It**

Once you're measuring TDI quarter after quarter, it becomes a treasure trove of information.

- Is your company's TDI trending up or down?
- What is your sales TDI versus your marketing TDI?
- What is the TDI of your senior-leadership team versus your middle managers?
- Is your TDI highest in your core functions (functions that differentiate you in the marketplace)?
- Which leaders are consistently growing their TDI? What can other leaders learn from this?
- Which leaders are struggling with their TDI? How can you help them?
- What actions seem to have the biggest impact on your TDI?

## BURNING QUESTIONS

**What's considered a good TDI?**
There's no magic answer to this question. The number itself is less important than the act of using it as a benchmark and taking actions to improve it.

Many teams start with a negative (below zero) TDI—and it scares the crap out of them, as it should. If that's you, I understand. Be brave. You have to know and accept your current state in order to begin a path to change it for the better.

**What if my TDI is very high? Does that mean I don't need to take any action to improve it?**
If your TDI is a very high positive number, there's still work to do! A high TDI means a majority of your team members are performing at a high level. Congratulations... now it's time to raise the bar. Remember, high-performing team members want to be challenged. Challenging them by adding new responsibilities or raising their productivity expectations might temporarily lower your TDI, but it's ultimately an important step in your growth as a team.

## Quick Review

We're doing the wrong things to drive accountability:

- We have no clear definition of accountability.
- Team member performance assessment and improvement is a lone effort.
- Human resources is viewed too tactically.
- There isn't a way available to understand or measure strength of talent.

We need to hold leaders accountable for the following:

- Assessing the performance of their team accurately
- Taking action with each direct report
- Raising the bar
- Providing feedback on peers' direct reports
- Increasing the talent density of their team

The quarterly talent assessment meeting (QTAM) is the truth serum and the driver of accountability that focuses on strengthening talent each quarter.

If you don't measure strength of talent, you won't have strength of talent.

The Talent Density Indicator (TDI) is calculated as:

**TDI = High Performing % – (Low Producing % + Low Culture Fit %)**

Use the TDI:

- As a benchmark and to set quarterly targets
- As a gauge of the truth
- To establish ownership
- To learn from it

Go to my website strengthoftalent.com to access my book resources, where you'll find the Talent Assessment Form used in the quarterly talent assessment meeting.

To help better hold yourself and team members accountable for actions as well as automating the calculation of the Talent Density Indicator (TDI), go to talentdensitysystems.com to learn about this system and claim your free three-month access to the tool.

STEP 5

# CASCADE

## What's Next

Nope! You didn't miss a section. I know I've started each new step with a "The Wrong Way" section. But you're not doing it wrong if you're not doing it at all!

Whether you've followed along and completed the exercises as you read, or have read the book without stopping to do the work, you're probably asking, "What's next?"

Cascading this process down or up your organization can start with you no matter what role you play in your firm: CEO, business owner, member of a leadership team, team leader, or a team member with *no* direct reports... yet.

### For CEOs/Business Owners

Follow these steps for cascading actions down through your organization:

1. Begin by setting the right productivity and culture fit expectations for your direct reports—collaboratively with your team, if possible. These will never be perfect, so you do the best you can and know they will be refined as a normal part of their evolution. The key is to start and not get stuck trying to get it right the first time. It will not be right the first time, so set that as an expectation initially. Review Step 1 for the process steps. Moving forward, this step should happen as needed. You don't need to reset expectations each quarter. However, reviewing them

quarterly will determine if they still are appropriate or if changes are needed.

2. Assess your direct reports based on these expectations. Review Step 2 for the process steps. If possible, review this assessment with someone you trust outside of your organization—a coach, a mentor, or accountability partner. It's important to have someone challenge your thinking and ensure you're not being too easy or too hard on your team. Calculate the Talent Density Indicator (TDI) for your team, in Step 4. Use it as a benchmark and set a TDI goal for next quarter. Take this step every quarter.

3. Define the actions you're committing to take for each of your direct reports. Define actions quarterly and review them throughout the quarter (by yourself and in your one-on-ones with your direct reports) to determine if changes are needed. Review Step 3 for specific recommendations. Reviewing these actions with a coach, mentor, or accountability partner will help to challenge your thinking. As above, it's helpful to use a coach or accountability partner to help hold you accountable for taking these actions.

4. Schedule and begin conducting weekly one-on-one meetings (or biweekly to start, if building a new one-on-one habit) with each direct report using the one-on-one meeting framework in Step 3.

5. Once comfortable with this process (likely after one or two quarters), cascade this process down to your leadership team. This will be covered more in the next section.

**For Members of the Senior Leadership Team**

Follow steps one to four from "For CEOs/Business Owners," above.

Either in parallel with those steps or after you've completed them, share this process with your CEO and leadership team. Having them read the book might be a great start (yes, help me sell more books!). Implementing this process just for your team will have great value. However, implementing it across the organization will be exponentially more powerful by ensuring your great team gets to work with other great teams.

### For Team Leaders

Follow steps one to four from "For CEOs/Business Owners."

Either in parallel with those steps or after you've completed them, share this process with your leader. Of course, having them read the book might be a great start. Again, implementing this process just for your team will have great value. However, implementing it across the organization will be exponentially more powerful.

### For Team Members with No Direct Reports

If you've made it through this book (well, almost) and you don't have direct reports yet, congratulations for being ambitious enough to learn this content, as it will make you a better team member and better leader in the days to come!

Start by engaging your manager to ensure their expectations of you for both culture fit and productivity are defined and clear. There are two goals for you here: first, to understand what's expected of you as the initial step to being successful in your role, and second, to have a chance to teach your leader some ideas from this book. And, of course, here comes the shameless plug to share my book with your leader, in the hopes that they can help drive implementing this process throughout your organization.

### For Everyone

Regardless of where you start, focus on the outcomes that naturally occur as a result of implementing this process. What will it look like when this process is fully implemented throughout your organization?

- You will have a team filled with only high performers.
- You will be surrounded by people who consistently challenge you to be at your best.

**There's no such thing as a successful rollout** of a mediocre process.

---

- You will work with people who are just as self-motivated as you.

- You won't have to micromanage low-performing team members that aren't improving.

- Your company will become a talent magnet for high performers.

- Your team will be so effective that your biggest challenge will be how high to raise the bar on their next set of goals.

### The Top-Down Approach

Since the more typical implementation of this framework will start at or near the top of the organization, I want to share a philosophy that will be helpful in envisioning how this could cascade down through your organization.

*Get it right at the top before you cascade it to the bottom.*

Why? Because there's no such thing as a successful rollout of a mediocre process.

That means you may decide to use this process as a leadership team (meaning, the CEO and the leadership team are using this framework to assess and take action with and for their direct reports) for several quarters before you decide to cascade it down to the next level in your organization.

Here's what that might look like (you might decide to speed up or slow down your actual implementation).

### Quarter 1

The CEO begins using this process to set expectations for, assess, and take action with the leadership team. I often start this process with CEOs before they've effectively defined productivity expectations for each of their direct reports. They simply score productivity between 1 and 10 as best they can. While it's preferable to have specific productivity expectations, this is not a bad way to start the process, so they don't get bogged down in details.

The QTAM might take the form of the CEO reviewing their assessments and actions with a coach, mentor, or accountability partner.

### Quarter 3

After executing the process for two quarters, the CEO cascades the process down to their direct reports on the leadership team. The leadership team is now asked to set expectations for, assess, and take action with their teams.

There will now be two QTAMs:

1. The leadership team QTAM will be attended by the CEO and the leadership team, giving the leadership team a chance to collaborate and hold each other accountable.

2. The CEO will still conduct a mini-QTAM with a coach, mentor, or accountability partner to discuss their leadership team.

If you have three levels of team members (CEO, leadership team, and team members), that's all the cascading that's required. By cascading down to the leadership team, every team member is now touched by the process.

However, if you have more than three levels of team members (for example, CEO, leadership team, directors, managers, team members), additional cascading is necessary.

For example...

### Quarter 6

After executing the process with the leadership team for three quarters, it is decided (by the VP of sales, in collaboration with the CEO) that the VP of sales is ready to cascade the process down to their direct reports on the sales team. The sales directors are now asked to set expectations for, assess, and take action with their teams. There will now be three QTAMs:

1. The sales team QTAM will be attended by the VP of sales and sales directors.

2. The leadership team QTAM will be attended by the CEO and the leadership team, giving the leadership team a chance to collaborate and hold each other accountable.

3. The CEO will still conduct a mini-QTAM with a coach, mentor, or accountability partner to discuss their leadership team.

I've seen organizations decide to cascade down to this third level of leadership all at once (all leaders cascade it down to their next level of leadership) or one team at a time, as in my previous example with the VP of sales. Both can work; however, I'm partial to the "one team at a time" method, because not every leader is ready at the same time. Here are some ways to gauge whether a leader is "ready":

- Is the leader performing at least at a medium level?
- Does the leader fully agree with and commit to the process?
- Does the leader understand the process at a deep enough level that they can facilitate their own QTAM with their team?
- Are they effectively taking action with their direct reports to improve strength of talent, including regular one-on-one meetings?
- Are their leaders performing at a medium level or higher?

My coaching is to take this slow. When we try to implement change quickly and widely within our organization, we can end up confusing and frustrating everyone—and sometimes even making things worse than they were before the change.

*Sometimes we have to slow things down to speed things up.*

While this may feel like a longer process, the road to real value is much shorter than if you screw it up five times before you get it right. Cascading too quickly can result in inaccurate assessments, actions that add little or no value, and, more importantly, fear and resistance from an organization that may misunderstand the process and its benefits.

## Proactively Manage the Change

Change management and clear communication are paramount in cascading this framework through the organization.

We need to make sure that leaders see value in the process for the business and their teams, and are comfortable being open and vulnerable about the performance of their direct reports. For many, their natural reaction will be to protect their people and themselves: "Why should I assess someone as low performing? It just shines the spotlight on me and causes me to do extra work. I may be challenged to have a difficult conversation I don't want to have. Or worse, I may be challenged to fire someone and then I'll be short-staffed." Or, "Wow, we have a lot of low performers, will there be mass firings when we start doing this?" If your leaders view this process negatively, perceptions will only get worse as you cascade this through the organization.

While this process is not one that needs to be introduced with great fanfare, we also don't want to assume we can keep it a secret. We need to assume that team members will find out something different is happening. They'll hear their leaders talking about a new type of quarterly meeting or wonder why their leader scheduled a meeting with them to "review expectations." If we're not careful, people will make up their own stories... and they're almost never good.

To that end, we also need to make sure all members of the organization, leaders and individual team members, understand the purpose of the process and view it positively: "Did you hear? All the leaders huddle in a conference room once a quarter to figure out who they're going to fire." Or, "All they do is look at numbers now. It's like we're not people anymore." Ouch! An organization

**Get it right at the top** before you cascade it to the bottom.

---

that views this process negatively can create much more harm than good. The Talent Density System should improve not only performance but morale and employee retention as well. Not paying attention to the change management component can result in the opposite. Team members need to see clearly how this process benefits them personally, not just how it benefits the team or company.

To help leaders and team members take ownership and become fully engaged in the process, we need to ensure they internalize the purpose of the process as well as the benefits of improving their performance. We also need to make people part of the process. After all, this is being done *for* them, not *to* them.

### Ingrain the Purpose of the Process

Ingrain means to establish something, such as a belief, so firmly that it is not likely to change. That's much deeper than just understanding.

There are three powerful ways to ingrain the purpose.

1. **Define the purpose, clearly and succinctly.**

    My purpose in creating the Talent Density System was to give leaders better tools to drive the growth of their team members, leading to profit growth with less frustration and greater fulfillment. My purpose focuses on leaders because that's my primary audience.

    Your purpose needs to focus on *all* team members. It might be "To allow our leaders and team members to better work together to improve themselves and the company." Or it could be "To allow our company to reach *its* potential by helping all of our team members reach *their* potential."

    The leadership team must align on a purpose that's simple, succinct, and measurable. A three-paragraph purpose will never be remembered, never repeated in the same way, and never truly be ingrained.

2. **Tell stories that affirm the purpose.**
Left up to the individual, stories about the process might be disempowering or empowering. A disempowering story might sound like this: "Once a quarter our leaders huddle in a conference to rate us and decide if we're a fit." An empowering story might sound like this: "What an amazing set of leaders we work for! They're constantly working together on ways they can help us be more successful."

Once you align on a purpose, find and create opportunities to tell stories that affirm that purpose. Quarterly town hall meetings, weekly team meetings, one-on-one meetings, and more informal discussions are all opportunities to tell empowering stories.

Stories can focus on messages such as:

- Individual team members who have dramatically improved their performance
- Powerful leaders who have dramatically improved team performance through effective coaching and development
- Successful company results that can be attributed back to the performance improvement of individual team members
- Improved team member engagement or retention
- The many benefits of not having to conduct annual reviews anymore

3. **Model behavior that affirms the purpose.**
Leaders must live and model the purpose every day. The best way to do that is to embrace meaningful actions and execute the process with discipline.

- Make development of your team members your number one priority
- Set clear expectations with your team members, holding them accountable to those expectations

- Review action plans with your team members to help them improve their performance
- Conduct consistent one-on-one meetings focused on coaching, accountability, and feedback
- Give frequent, real-time feedback… don't wait for your next one-on-one
- Have difficult discussions instead of avoiding them
- Model culture fit by living the core values consistently

If your actions are not congruent with the purpose, team members will stop believing and start telling disempowering stories—to themselves and others.

### Promote the Benefits of the Process

"What's in it for me?" That's not a selfish question; it's human nature to be curious. Therefore, in addition to ingraining the purpose, we need to help both leaders and team members understand how they'll benefit from being part of the process. These benefits can and should be communicated formally, in addition to being reinforced more informally in conversation and through stories. These may help promote the benefits.

As a leader, this process will help you accomplish essential goals:

- Drive your success by increasing the strength of your team
- Enhance your impact as a leader as you help others to succeed
- Reduce your level of overwhelm and frustration with your team
- Improve your ability to assess talent, coach talent, develop talent
- Know how and when to make the tough decision to transition someone who's not a strong fit out of the organization
- Increase your ability to focus on more strategic tasks

As one of our team members, this process will help you accomplish essential goals:

- Feel more in control by knowing exactly what's expected of you
- Know exactly what actions to take to improve your performance
- Improve your chances of success with the help of more regular coaching and feedback
- Feel challenged to learn and improve every day
- Be more in control of your future career path, inside or outside the company

**Encourage Leadership Openness and Vulnerability**

Early in the implementation of this framework, leaders will have the tendency to protect their people. They'll protect them out of loyalty or fear. Assessing someone as "low producing" or "low culture fit" will result in a challenge to do something about it. They may need to have a difficult conversation they'd rather not have. Or fire someone they feel loyal to. Or be short-staffed when they already feel stretched too thin.

Here are some ways to encourage leaders to be more open and vulnerable about the performance of their team members:

1 Communicate the benefits of the process to leaders consistently — what's in it for them. The actions they need to take may feel awkward in the short term but will open a world of opportunity and possibility in the mid and long term.

2 Reinforce to leaders that everyone can be high performing... somewhere (see Step 3).

3 Incentivize leaders not just on their Talent Density Indicator but on their level of TDI improvement. In other words, leaders who have improved their TDI from 5 percent to 25 percent should be celebrated as much as, or more than, a leader who's been at a 45 percent TDI for the last three quarters.

4 Think about going a bit lighter on the "coach out" conversations for the first few quarters. In Step 3, I emphasized giving

leaders three months to coach a low-performing team member—if they couldn't coach them up in that time, they needed to coach them out. Early in the implementation of this process, leaders won't be great coaches. They won't be masters of having difficult conversations. It may take them a bit longer to effectively coach someone toward stronger performance or to make the decision that they don't fit. Giving leaders an extra three months (but no longer than that!) during the first few quarters to allow time to hone their experience might reduce any anxiety.

### Gamify the Process

A great friend of mine is obsessed with his Oura Ring. Every day he tries to get better sleep to maximize his "resilience score" and "readiness score," and to optimize his resting heart rate. It's not about the ring judging him: "You're a crappy sleeper." The ring provides his scores and helps understand what actions he can take to improve them. He's motivated by those scores because he knows making these improvements will help him create a better life.

He's not alone. Millions of people across the world are motivated by health apps. Did you ever walk around your house for fifteen minutes just so you could hit ten thousand steps before you went to bed? We've gamified our health. With access to current performance scores on our productivity and culture fit measures, why can't we do the same thing for our team members?

### Help Your Team Members "Win the Game"

We want to play a game when we have a chance to win. We know where the finish line is, we know how to get there, and we're motivated to get there.

Here are some ways to help your team members win the game:

- Increase transparency on productivity measures. While I don't recommend sharing the performance category your team members are in ("Joe, you're low producing"), I absolutely recommend sharing and discussing productivity measures as frequently as possible with team members. If team members understand where they are versus expectations, they can own doing something about it.

- Help team members understand the leading indicators. These are measures of behaviors that drive results. If a salesperson needs to improve their new revenue by 20 percent (a lagging indicator), they might do it by increasing the number of meetings with decision-makers by 40 percent. Or by increasing the number of times they're asking for referrals by 50 percent. These leading indicators are tangible behaviors we can impact. If someone is not consistently living our collaboration core value, what leading indicators will allow them to raise their score in that area? Maybe it's how often they're offering their help to another team member.

- Incentivize growth, not just performance. Don't just incentivize the people that are performing the best, incentivize the people that are improving the most. This goes for individuals and their performance scores, and for leaders striving to improve their Talent Density Indicator.

- Stop using nominalization when driving performance. Nominalization is using a noun for something that's really an action (and thus should be a verb). "Productivity" is a nominalization. It sounds like a static thing. "Your productivity is low" subtly sounds static and unchangeable. A more powerful way to convey this is, "You need to produce more." That makes it sound like the outcome is changeable, and less like you're labeling someone. "Collaboration" is another nominalization. "You need to improve your collaboration" sounds nebulous. "You need to collaborate more and better" almost sounds like something you can do, with some help.

- Use the term "current score" every time. "Your current client retention score is 15 percent below goal" sends the message that this is a dynamic thing. It also sends a message that I, as your leader, am assuming you have the potential to improve. "Your current score is low" sends a message that it's not about you; it's just what your score is right now.

- Help team members understand how their performance impacts the team and the company's ability to reach its goals and vision. For example:

  - Achieving our accounts receivable goals allows us to meet our cash flow targets and invest in our new warehouse.

  - Having a new warehouse will allow us to improve on-time shipping to clients and dramatically improve client retention.

  - Improving client retention will allow us to achieve our growth goals, leading to larger bonuses and more opportunities for our team members.

## Critical Roles

Cascading the Talent Density System through the organization and handling the challenges along the way require one more important element: an understanding of everyone's role in the process.

This involves determining *who* is accountable for the success of these efforts throughout the organization. While the answer may differ depending on the size and structure of your organization, here are my recommendations.

**The CEO/business owner** is the champion of the efforts to improve strength of talent across the organization. That means it's critical that they embrace these key practices:

- Believe in and communicate the importance of this process throughout the organization. This communication needs to happen frequently, consistently, and perpetually—not just once when the process is introduced.

- Model the behavior required to effectively execute the program. That means setting expectations, assessing performance, and acting and driving accountability at the highest level. That means ensuring they set up one-on-one meetings with each of their direct reports and have difficult conversations when warranted. If they aren't diligent in their execution of the process, others in the organization will use it as an excuse to do the same.

**The VP of HR/talent development** is accountable for improving the strength of talent across the organization. That means it's critical that they embrace these key practices:

- Ensure that the processes, tools, and templates required for successful implementation are available and understood
- Hold themselves accountable for the overall Talent Density Indicator (TDI) for the organization
- Define quarterly TDI targets for the organization
- Work with each leadership team member as needed to support the implementation of the process with their teams

**Leadership team members** are accountable for the strength of talent on their teams and are responsible for improving the strength of talent across the organization. That means it's critical that they embrace these key practices:

- Ensure that the processes, tools, and templates required for successful implementation are adopted and utilized by their team members
- Hold themselves accountable for the TDI for their team
- Define quarterly TDI targets for their team
- Work with each of their team members as needed to support the implementation of the process
- Work with other leadership team members to assist in the efforts to improve the strength of talent across the organization

**Team leaders** are accountable for the strength of talent on their team. That means it's critical that they embrace these key practices:

- Ensure they're utilizing the processes, tools, and templates required to improve the strength of talent on their team
- Hold themselves accountable for the TDI for their team
- Define quarterly TDI targets for their team
- Work with each of their team members, as required, to support the implementation of the process

**Team members** are accountable for their own results and helping others do the same. That means it's critical that they embrace these key practices:

- Understand and align with what's expected of them from the perspectives of both culture fit and productivity. It's important they hold their leaders accountable for collaborating or, at least, sharing this information
- Understand how their performance expectations link to the company's goals
- Know how they're doing against those expectations. It's important they hold their leaders accountable for making this information available
- Ask for coaching, feedback, and accountability
- Ensure their leader is having weekly (or, at first, biweekly) one-on-one meetings with them
- Help and collaborate with other team members who are striving to achieve their own results

> **BURNING QUESTIONS**
>
> **What if I don't have a head of HR or talent management?**
> If you're at a stage in your company's growth where you haven't justified having an HR or talent management role, their accountabilities can be assumed either by the CEO or by another leadership team member. Depending on the size or maturity of your organization, it may be time to rethink whether you need to add the function to your leadership team. Remember, the #1 driver of profit growth is people growth. Who, in your organization, has the expertise and time to drive that effort?

## Quick Review

If you're a CEO or business owner, your next steps are:

- Start the process yourself by setting expectations, assessing performance, and taking actions with and for your leadership team
- Cascade the process to your leadership team (so they can do the same for their direct reports) once you're comfortable with it

If you're a senior leadership team member, your next steps are:

- Start the process yourself by setting expectations, assessing performance, and taking actions with and for your team
- Share this process with your CEO and leadership team

If you're a team leader, your next steps are:

- Start the process yourself by setting expectations, assessing performance, and taking actions with and for your team
- Share this process with your leader

If you're a team member with no direct reports, your next steps are:

- Ensure you're clear as to the expectations, related to both culture fit and productivity, your leader has for you
- Share this process with your leader

Take the top-down approach to rolling out this process to your organization. To proactively manage the change, let's review the following steps:

- You need change management and clear communication to cascade this framework to the organization.
- Your challenges are:
  - Fear and resistance from the organization
  - Leaders protecting their team members
- Your strategies to overcome the challenges include:
  - Ingrain the purpose of the process
  - Promote the benefits of the process
  - Encourage leadership openness and vulnerability
  - Gamify the process
  - Help your team members win the game

The critical roles required for successful implementation of the process are:

- CEO/business owner as champion
- VP of HR/talent development as accountable for overall results
- Leadership team members as accountable for their team's results and responsible for overall results
- Team leaders as accountable for their team's results
- Team members as accountable for their own results and helping others achieve results

To help better hold yourself and team members accountable for actions as well as automating the calculation of the TDI, go to talentdensitysystems.com to learn about this system and claim your free three-month access to the tool.

# NOW WHAT?

A T THE BEGINNING of this book, I made you promises. Did I hold true to those promises? Only you can truly answer that, but let's check!

I promised that by reading this book you will reap the following benefits:

**Appreciate the impact of putting a higher priority on assessing, coaching, and developing your direct reports much more frequently.**
I hope you connected with the research and client stories throughout the book showing you the impact of executing these ideas in the real world.

**Know how and when to make the tough decision to transition someone who's not a strong fit out of the organization.**
You now have several techniques for acting on team members who are performing below expectations, including how and when to make the decision to coach a team member out of the organization.

**Develop clearer expectations for each of your direct reports.**
The Talent Density Expectations Model gives you the framework you need to set expectations for productivity as well as culture fit.

**Assess the performance of your direct reports using those expectations.**
The Talent Assessment Model gives you the ability to assess talent along the two expectation-setting components of culture fit and productivity.

**Define a clear set of actions for each of your direct reports based on that assessment.**
You now have specific actions for each level of performance, as well as more general actions to level up the performance of your team. You understand how to have difficult conversations and were introduced to a one-on-one meeting framework to drive ongoing communication and action for each member of your team.

**Create a measurable benchmark for the strength of talent on your team, so you can measure and hold yourself accountable for improvement.**
You understand the importance of holding leaders accountable for building the strength of talent on their teams, and have two powerful tools to implement that accountability: The TDI and the QTAM.

**Craft a plan to implement this framework throughout your organization.**
You have guidance on the top-down approach, strategies to overcome the potential challenges along the way, and an understanding of the important roles necessary to drive implementation across all teams.

NOW THAT I'VE kept my promises, what promises are you willing to make? Here are some ideas to get you started:

- Set clearer expectations for each of your team members.
- Assess performance against those expectations.
- Take massive action with and for each of your direct reports, regardless of their level of performance.

- Have the difficult discussions you've been postponing.
- Schedule and execute on an improved framework for one-on-one meetings with your direct reports.
- If you're the CEO: Share this book with your direct reports and schedule your first QTAM to drive accountability.
- If you're not the CEO: Share this book with your peers and your CEO. Persist until they schedule your first QTAM to drive accountability.
- Calculate your TDI. Use this as a benchmark and set goals for next quarter.

Remember, the #1 driver of profit growth is people growth. Make people growth your number one priority and reach your goals:

- Increase top- and bottom-line growth
- Create a growing, fulfilling work environment
- Create greater value for your clients and other stakeholders
- Increase your trust that the team can get the job done, with or without you
- Be able to successfully take on new, exciting opportunities
- Be able to successfully take on greater challenges

To help you take action and achieve the incredible impact I've described in the book, here's one last chance to head to strengthoftalent.com and check out the myriad resources I've created to help you on your journey.

Go get 'em!!

# ACKNOWLEDGMENTS

FIRST, AND MOST IMPORTANTLY, I need to thank my amazing wife Angela, son Richie, and daughter Jessica. They put up with me through my constant travel schedule and incessant jabbering about my work and clients—I can get pretty obsessed.

I'd like to thank Keith Cupp, the outstanding president of Gravitas Impact Premium Coaches and a leader with the biggest heart I know. His teaching, coaching, and mentoring laid the groundwork for much of my work today.

Thanks also to my business coach of many years, the incredible David Herdlinger. I'm a better person every time I leave one of our many coaching calls.

My mastermind groups have known exactly when to pat me on the back, kick me in the ass, or knock my brain into a more creative gear. To Owen Fitzpatrick, Cait Donovan, Sean Evans, Doug Diamond, Jeff Dorman, and my amazing CEO roundtable at the Commerce and Industry Association of New Jersey, I thank you.

Thank you Xime Duarte for becoming so much more than the "assistant" I hired in 2022. You have become an indispensable part of my team.

I want to thank the incredibly talented folks at Brand Builders Group led by Rory Vaden and AJ Vaden, and my amazing brand strategist, Kristen Hartnagel.

Thank you to the super-talented group at Page Two, who have guided me through the book writing process every step of the way.

And, last, but certainly not least, I want to thank my clients. Throughout my more than thirty-five years as a consultant and coach, you have challenged me to be my best and helped me create the business I love.

PHOTO: JOHN DEMATO

# ABOUT THE AUTHOR

MIKE GOLDMAN is a leadership team coach; the bestselling author of two books, *Breakthrough Leadership Team* and *Performance Breakthrough*; and host of *The Better Leadership Team Show* podcast. He's a TEDx speaker, and presents internationally to groups of business leaders, such as the Young Presidents' Organization, Vistage, Women Presidents Organization, TEC Canada, and the Entrepreneurs' Organization. During his thirty-five-year coaching and consulting career, he has worked with clients including Disney, Verizon, Chanel, and Polo Ralph Lauren. His insights have been featured in *Forbes*, *Fast Company*, and *Chief Executive* magazine.

## Want some help taking the next step in building the strength of talent in your organization?

---

Here are some shameless plugs… I mean, ways to accelerate your progress.

**Buy copies of this book for all leaders within your organization**
Want to buy books for the leaders in your organization?
Email me at mike@mike-goldman.com for bulk discounts and special offers.

**Schedule a Talent Density Launchpad**
The most powerful way to launch this process in your organization is through the immersion of a half-day or full-day workshop. Go to mike-goldman.com/talent-density-launchpad to schedule a call to learn more.

**Bring me in to speak to your company, industry organization, or conference**
Do you believe others in your organization or industry group would get value from the ideas in this book?
Go to mike-goldman.com/speaking to find out more, or schedule a call.

**Leverage the Talent Density Systems web-based application**
The Talent Density Systems web-based application will help maximize your ability to set expectations, assess performance, document actions, and hold yourself and your team accountable for improving the strength of talent in your organization. For more information on how to implement it for your team, go to talentdensitysystems.com.

**Leverage these concepts to create a great leadership team**
When I'm not writing or speaking, I'm coaching leadership teams. If you want to take your leadership team to the next level, check out my previous book by going to mike-goldman.com/break-through-leadership-team, or to find out more about my leadership team coaching, go to mike-goldman.com/coaching.

## What clients have said about the Talent Density System

"Our leadership team has been using the Talent Density System to gauge staff performance for years. It provides us with an objective tool to track trends in employee behavior and allows us to make staffing decisions based on concrete data rather than emotion. As a result, we've been able to successfully attract and retain highly productive, talented people who actively live our company's core values and help us continue to raise our business to the next level."

**SHARON MAROTTA**, CFO, Marotta Plastic Surgery Specialists

"The Talent Density System has become the core language our executives use to approach evaluating and developing people. We have seen tremendous growth in culture and morale, with better collaboration within and across teams and a meaningfully better employee experience overall."

**BRAM WALTERS**, CEO, SunVest Solar, LLC

"The Talent Density System has allowed my leadership team and me to objectively assess the performance and productivity of our staff. Being able to turn to numbers, instead of resorting to hunches or subjective experiences, has given us the power to have candid, constructive conversations with team members, and it has given us the confidence to make critical decisions."

**STEPHANIE HARRIS**, CEO, PartnerCentric

"Since integrating the Talent Density System into our operations, we've seen transformative changes. It has refined our approach to talent management, enabling us to focus intensely on fostering high performers while addressing areas where our team could improve. This has significantly enhanced our company's productivity and morale. It has also allowed me to delegate more confidently."

**CHAD STARK**, CEO, Stark Carpet

"The Talent Density System is the foundation for defining performance outcomes and core values/behaviors within our business. It (1) defines what great performance and cultural alignment looks like, (2) instills a consistent lexicon to discuss talent across our global business, and (3) provides focus on recruiting and retaining top talent while simultaneously taking action when outcomes or core values are not in alignment."

**TRICIA BRENN**, EVP of Talent, Logility

"The Talent Density System has allowed us to make necessary adjustments to elevate overall performance, and it revealed high-performing team members who deserved more attention and development opportunities. Team morale and productivity have surged, leading to improved client experience, revenue growth, and profitability. This clarity has also reduced my stress as a leader, enabling me to focus strategically on business growth."

**JOHN PECK**, CEO, PB Roofing